Cornell International Industrial and Labor Relations Report Number 19

POST ABOLISHED

One Woman's Struggle for Employment Rights in Tanzania

Laeticia Mukurasi

ILR Press
Ithaca, New York

Published in Great Britain by The Women's Press Ltd.

Jacket design by Sue Lamble

Library of Congress Cataloging-in-Publication Data

Mukurasi, Laeticia, 1951–
Post abolished : one woman's struggle for employment rights in Tanzania / Laeticia Mukurasi.
p. cm. — (Cornell international industrial and labor relations report ; no. 19)
"Published in Great Britain by the Women's Press Ltd."—T.p. verso.
Includes bibliographical references.
ISBN 0-87546-702-4 (alk. paper) : — ISBN 0-87546-703-2 (pbk. : alk. paper) :
1. Women—Employment—Tanzania. I. Title. II. Series: Cornell international industrial and labor relations reports ; no. 19.
HD6211.3.M85 1991
331.4'133'09678—dc20 91-18497

Copies may be ordered through bookstores or directly from
ILR Press
New York State School of Industrial and Labor Relations
Cornell University
Ithaca, NY 14853-3901

Printed on acid-free paper in the United States by Braun Brumfield

POST ABOLISHED

This book is dedicated to my parents
Melania Clara Kalikwendwa
and
Cornelius Peter Kabyemela,
my daughters
Kemilembe, Shubi and Karungi
and
to the Women of the World who
never surrender the struggle
To make the world a better place.

For the purposes of the present Convention, the term 'discrimination against Women' shall mean any distinction, exclusion or restriction made on the basis of sex which has the effect or purpose of impairing or nullifying the recognition, enjoyment or exercise by women, irrespective of their marital status, on a basis of equality of men and women, of human rights and fundamental freedoms in the political, economic, social, cultural, civil or any other field.

Part I, Article I of the United Nations Convention on the Elimination of All Forms of Discrimination against Women

Laeticia's story makes compelling reading – a woman determined to live by the rules in a situation where positional privilege was rife and accountability an unknown concept; a woman manager taking on an almost entirely male parastatal and learning that when men fight they hit below the belt.

But Laeticia won, and has survived in hope to encourage other women by her story.

Dr Kate Young, Fellow of the Institute of Development Studies, University of Sussex, and founder of the work on gender and development at the Institute; currently Director of Womankind (Worldwide), a development charity working to support women's organisations and self-help groups in developing countries.

Contents

Acknowledgments

Rarely is a work of this kind a one-woman effort.

First and foremost my thanks go to James Mwale of J. J. Mwale Advocates of Arusha Town without whose support in enabling me to keep a 'fighting space' there would not have been anything to write about. Secondly, my gratitude goes to members of the JUWATA branch of Fibreboards (Africa) Limited, for their complete backing of a member who belonged to the category of 'them', and to the District, Regional and National JUWATA functionaries who had to deal with my case. I would like to mention especially the Chairman of the Fibreboards (Africa) Limited JUWATA branch at Gershom Lwande for his commitment throughout the dispute.

My appreciation goes also to the participants and staff on the study course, Women, Men and Development, at the Institute of Development Studies in the University of Sussex, who listened to me patiently and raised many questions which helped me gain a deeper insight into the issues involved, particularly Charity Mwansa from Zambia, Mary Rusimbi and Lynne Ukio from Tanzania, Kumudhini Rosa from Sri Lanka, Noreen Mahmood from Pakistan, Naila Kabeer from the UK, Faustina Ward-Osborne from Guyana, Emelina Quintillan from the Philippines and Emmanuel Chiabi from Cameroon.

My thanks also to the women and men who came to wish me well after my reinstatement and who encouraged me to write about my experience. They insisted that my case illustrated more than just my own struggle and that the downtrodden everywhere would benefit from reading my story. For obvious reasons, those women and men who extended help to me while understanding and being aware of the hidden dimensions of my dispute will not be mentioned by name.

I am grateful to those who read the manuscript, correcting my English and demanding clarifications of unfamiliar expressions, especially Shuna Mason of Brighton; and to Jeorge Dyrkton of Canada and Sarla Campbell of the Institute of Development Studies at Sussex University who, in typing the manuscript, corrected and improved it.

My thanks go to the newspaper and radio journalists who managed to bring my dispute to public attention in an interesting and informative way, especially William Nchimbi and Hemed Kimwaga; to the Secretary General of the Tanzania Women's Union, Umoja wa Wanawake wa Tanzania; to the various people who donated food or money and those who sent me letters of encouragement even though we had never met; to my daughter Kemilembe and my househelp Abela Kyelengya and to my cousin George Rugaimukamu and my brother Bernard for their love and support at the most difficult time of my life.

Finally, I thank Daniel Kyaruzi, who continues to stand behind me and tell me that I am right.

Abbreviations

CCM	Chama cha Mapinduzi. Referred to as the Party.
ECA	Economic Commission for Africa
ESAMI	Eastern and Southern African Management Institute
FAL	Fibreboards (Africa) Limited
IBRD	International Bank for Reconstruction and Development
IMF	International Monetary Fund
JUWATA	Jumuia ya Wafanyakasi wa Tanzania: Tanzania Workers' Union. Referred to also as the Union.
PLT	Permanent Labour Tribunal
PLT Act	Permanent Labour Tribunal Act (Act No. 41 of 1967)
SCOPO	Presidential Standing Committee on Parastatal Organisations
TEXCO	Tanzania Textile Corporation
TWICO	Tanzania Wood Industry Corporation
UNIDO	United Nations Industrial Development Organisation
UWT	Umoja wa Wanawake wa Tanzania: Tanzania Women's Union. Referred to also as the Women's Organisation.

Introduction

Over a period of more than two years from February 1985 until mid-1987 I was involved in a trade dispute encompassing aspects of industrial relations, managerial decision-making, labour law, bureaucracy and women's rights in Tanzania. This book is my account of that personal experience. In it I depict my struggle to get reinstated in my job following dismissal disguised as in the national interest. The question was the extent to which my dismissal constituted an interest that could even remotely be interpreted as 'national'. All along I maintained that it was not. Finally, the Labour Tribunal agreed and ordered my reinstatement. Looking back now with a clearer perspective my case stands out as a classic example of an extension and glorification of those negative patriarchal values which seek to define women as members of the inferior sex within a sexual hierarchy and which accord women lower rank in terms of status, temperament and sex roles. For some individuals such beliefs are external givens, having almost the force of a religion. As we shall see, however, the inferiority accorded to women by the adherents of such views exists only in their minds and has no objective reality.

My case raises the kind of political issue to which women have been seeking answers for a long time: what is the basis for a lopsided distribution that gives more privileges to one sex at the expense of the other? To put it more clearly, it raises questions that involve conflict not only over the production and distribution of wealth, but also over the production and distribution of human dignity and respect, both of which favour men above women.

Recent writings about women have pointed out that it is women's silence that has rendered them invisible and because of this invisibility policies and plans meant to enhance the position of women have only been partially implemented. My intention here is to make visible to a wider audience a case which started as a private matter but was transformed into a very public issue within Tanzania. I hope that by speaking aloud my experience I may help create awareness and pave the way for change not just in Tanzania but elsewhere in the world too. In the process, I hope that my story will serve as a source of understanding and inspiration for women and men who have had similar experiences.

I have written this book with a number of objectives in mind. Firstly, I hope to show that though policies and legislation supporting equality between men and women exist in Tanzania, there are deep problems in trying to move from a position where legislation and policy are mere principles to one in which they are practised. Women's issues are still entangled with some deeply ingrained attitudes which have a socio-cultural base within Tanzanian society. While the prevailing Tanzanian political ideology endorses egalitarian ideals, social attitudes are still very much in consonance with a patriarchal value-system which espouses notions of male superiority and female inferiority. In other words, it appears that some individuals, steeped as they are in traditional values, cannot easily catch up with the egalitarian ideology. Tanzania's adoption of a policy of socialism and self-reliance in 1967 was intended to sound a death knell to the unequal treatment of women. For, to quote from the writing of the former President, Julius K. Nyerere:

> . . . it is true that women in traditional society were regarded as having a place in the community which was not only different but was also to some extent inferior . . . by virtue of their sex they suffered from inequalities which had nothing to do with their contribution to the family welfare. Although it is wrong to suggest that they have always been an oppressed group, it is true that within the traditional society, ill-treatment and enforced subservience could be their lot. This is certainly inconsistent with our socialist conception of the equality of all human beings and the rights of all to live in such security and freedom; for all progress now, it is essential that our women live in terms of full equality with their fellow citizens who are men. (Nyerere, 1973)

And in an instructive speech given in 1974 Nyerere said:

> Socialism is not possible without democracy, any more than it is possible without full acceptance of human equality regardless of race, tribe, religion or sex.

There is a well-known truism that old habits die hard. Indeed, studies have shown that social behaviour deeply rooted in tradition does not change rapidly. This case study clearly illustrates that mere formulation of policy or law will not do away with negative but popular stereotypes about women. Education and the opportunity to put policy and legislation into practice in society are necessary before real change can be effected. Special efforts have to be made to inculcate both men and women with a new attitude towards equality, and a genuine understanding of the new socialist morality. Mere exhortation or rhetoric without concrete results cannot be expected to soften the heart of an avowed male chauvinist or give vigour to the woman who lacks self-confidence or feminist consciousness.

Secondly, the book is intended to highlight the fact that policies and laws designed to promote equal rights for women form only one strand in a multiplicity of social policies and legislation. If there are anomalies in the formulation or implementation of these generally applicable policies and laws there is likely to be a corresponding deficiency in the way policies and laws designed to enhance the rights of women are expressed and put into practice. It is also true to say that women's rights may fail to be observed precisely *because* women are perceived socially, politically and economically as disadvantaged or vulnerable groups. Neither individually nor even collectively do women have enough clout to put policies and legislation designed for their benefit to best use. Most policy and law implementors are men, and women remain dependent on them and at their mercy.

Thirdly, since the locus of this dispute is a company in state ownership, and given the fact that, since the 1967 nationalisations, many firms in Tanzania are publicly owned, the book will show the extent to which the burden of policy implementation is borne by the state and by institutions specifically created to put its policies into practice. It will also touch on the role of the individual decision-makers who have to make decisions every day in the course of implementing government policies. Indeed policy implementation is a decision-making process. In my view my case is a good example of the kinds of problems involved in putting government policies and laws into practice.

The questions raised by my case also have a broader political, economic, social and cultural context which needs to be addressed. Since the late 1970s Tanzania has been experiencing a serious economic crisis, the most celebrated symptom of which is an acute shortage of foreign exchange. This state of affairs cannot be wholly blamed on external causes, attractive as that excuse may be. Domestic factors which have far-reaching ramifications have an adverse effect on the way precious, hard-earned foreign exchange is used. One example is the mismanagement and misuse of skilled manpower which makes it difficult for many highly skilled and patriotic Tanzanians, men and women, to give of their best. The recently observed brain drain of highly qualified Tanzanians to other countries is only one indicator. As a result our scarce foreign exchange is used to import foreigners with skills that, with good management and realistic incentive structures, could be found locally.

Another domestic problem results from unhealthy alliances, collusion, and the practice of nepotism involving highly placed bureaucrats in government service on one hand and the state-owned sector or parastatals on the other, and based on the 'You scratch my back, I'll scratch yours' dictum. It is because of such practices that some people who are not necessarily the best who could be found for the purpose have been appointed to top decision-making positions, in areas way beyond their competence, with disastrous results for the economy. Since such connections have been in existence for a long time, and since all the members of this bureaucracy know each other quite well, it becomes very difficult for them to engage in any constructive self-criticism. It would be unimaginable that they should criticise one another.

These two aspects – namely, the frustration of highly qualified and competent manpower on one hand and the appointment and retention of unsuitable elements in the top echelons of the state bureaucracy based on collusion, godfatherism and nepotism on the other – have led to situations of gross malpractice, inefficiency and failure to enforce accountability. If policies concerning equality between the sexes have to be handled in such an unhealthy environment, then observance of such rights cannot be guaranteed. As will become clear later on, such factors played an important part in my own protracted struggle.

Tanzania is one of the most poverty-stricken among the Least Developed Countries (LDCs) of Africa. The national economy has been deteriorating since the early 1970s but the deterioration had reached crisis proportions by the early 1980s, requiring radical readjustments. The import-substitution policies adopted under colonial rule have failed because it was difficult to continue with a high import content in manufacturing in a situation of chronic shortage of foreign exchange. The export-orientated policies have failed primarily because of the imbalance in value between what Tanzania exports and the goods it must import. The alternative 'Basic Need' strategies adopted in the 1980s fail because Tanzania has not generated and does not possess enough capacity in terms of technology, information and basic skills to enable it to produce enough to meet basic needs. The structural adjustment policies proposed by the International Monetary Fund (IMF), are currently beginning to have an impact.

Against this background, Tanzania needs to take measures to utilise economically and efficiently its indigenous resources to bring about a transformation. This is the cornerstone of the policy of socialism and self-reliance, adopted in 1967. Self-reliance, however, will not be served by the misuse and demoralisation of the work-force, whether female or male, and especially of highly skilled manpower, in the guise of the national interest. Twenty-five years after political independence, Tanzania is still to a certain extent dependent on foreign expertise, even though the attainment of self-sufficiency in manpower by 1980 has been the country's main objective since the first Five Year Development Plan of 1965. This objective is not made any more attainable by the adoption of a procedure whereby appointment and recruitment to top decision-making positions in such a critical sector as that of the parastatal organisations is done on the basis of 'technical know-who' (political patronage) instead of the more appropriate 'technical know-how'. Nor is self-reliance well served when there are no clear guidelines for accountability and when failure to be accountable goes unpunished. Politicians have the courage to tell the workers and peasants to tighten their belts to meet the challenge of the economic crises; a parallel requirement should be that bureaucrats are made to feel the consequences of any of their decisions which go against the national interest.

Within the broader context of the issues raised by my case it is important also to look at Tanzania's theoretical position on the woman question and to see how women actually fare in socialist Tanzania. Both nationally and internationally, Tanzania has won acclaim for its egalitarian stance.

At the international level, Tanzania, as a member of the United Nations, is a signatory to the International Development Strategy designed for the Third United Nations Development Decade, which provides, *inter alia*, that women participate fully and effectively in all aspects of economic development. Tanzania also participated in the formulation of, and agreed to implement, the forward-looking strategies for the advancement of women beyond the end of the United Nations Decade for Women. Enabling women to be effective agents, as well as beneficiaries of economic and social development, was singled out as a major objective of these strategies. Moreover, Tanzania is also a signatory to the Lomé Convention and has committed itself to the Lagos Plan of Action, both of which call for proper and effective utilisation of the nation's indigenous resources, including manpower, that is, both men and women. In addition, Tanzania has ratified the International Labour Organisation Convention that stresses *inter alia* the integration of women at meaningful levels of employment. Finally, Tanzania ratified the United Nations Convention on the elimination of all forms of discrimination against women. The Convention urges state parties to take all appropriate measures to eliminate discrimination against women in the field of employment, especially job security and all benefits and conditions of service.

At the national level, Tanzania's policy of socialism and self-reliance has given rise to unprecedented possibilities for the emancipation of women. The concept of self-reliance draws attention to the optimal use of the indigenous resources in a country where women make up more than 51 per cent of the population. The Ujamaa villages (communal villages) provide a forum where women and men work side by side, and earn income in their own right. Such a development may have implications for the distribution of resources and power relations between men and women, and presents possibilities for the growth of political consciousness among women.

As far as legislation is concerned, Tanzania is ahead of many countries in the world*. However, unless there is a total transformation of society, such laws can only have a fragmentary and piecemeal effect, reflecting the fragmented socio-cultural and neo-colonial economic environment in which such policies have to be practised. Thus, for example, the Employment Ordinance was revised in 1975 to stress those rights that pertain to women as employees. There was, however, no corresponding attempt to incorporate within the same Act a recognition of the fact that men also have family responsibilities and, as fathers, have certain obligations to fulfil. The law perpetuates the same inherent bias that accords responsibility for child-care to mothers alone. In this case both legislation and policy conform to the pre-1967 era; they fail to address themselves to sexual division of labour in the home which imposes a double day on women, and they dismally fail to encourage a sharing of domestic responsibilities. Clearly, full equality between the sexes is not being furthered through the existence

* see appendix

of this law. Effective incorporation of women as a labour force, however, demands that the sexual division of labour in the home must change. Such a lopsided view inherent in policies and legislation extends to other areas too. Provision of child-care facilities for working mothers is still unsatisfactory and inadequate. When one confronts public-sector employers with the request for such facilities, the excuse is that funds are inadequate. Yet posh new clubs designed to cater for the interests of male bureaucrats proliferate in the capital city and other towns.

How have women fared under socialism in Tanzania? Theoretically, very well. At least there is recognition on the statute books to which one may have recourse. Some countries are only just beginning to contemplate such a situation. Educationally there has been an unprecedented increase in the number of girls in all institutions of learning. The government has taken a positive decision to see that women are not under-represented, by, for example, lowering the pass mark to enable girls to obtain places at secondary school level, and adopting the Musoma Resolution which waived the requirement for girls to work for two years before entering university. However, women still make up less than 20 per cent of all students in the highest institutions of learning, and too many women still specialise in liberal arts subjects.

In terms of political representation, in 1987 20 per cent of all ministerial positions were held by women. In a previous predominantly male Parliament, the state set aside 15 seats for women representatives. There is, however, only one woman member in the Central Committee which is one of the highest policy-making organs in the country, and only one woman Principal Secretary.

Despite these efforts, in practice the position of women is far from being equal to that of men. The discussion here is limited to women employees, not because women in other economic categories are less important, but because it is necessary to focus on the central issues which this book is written to address. It is possible, however, that some aspects of the discussion may be relevant to women in other economic categories, if not in terms of substance, then in terms of its more general effects.

Women employees comprise less than 10 per cent of the labour force. Of this 10 per cent most are marginalised and pushed into jobs that are unskilled, secretarial, clerical and of a temporary nature. Very few women can be found at the foreman and supervisory levels. They are also seriously under-represented at the managerial level, comprising less than 20 per cent of the total holding senior managerial positions. There are even fewer women as top executives. In my view, the main reason for the paucity of women at top levels is not necessarily that women have been disadvantaged in education and training. Women have been graduating from local and foreign institutions of higher education since 1970. If possession of relevant education and training were the main issue, some of the top male bureaucrats in Tanzania today would not occupy the positions they do, for they possess neither the academic qualifications nor the relevant experience for these executive positions. Some bureaucrats have acquired their posts through the 'old boy network' (inaccessible to most women) and 'technical know-who'.

By locating my arguments in the context of female employment, and using my own experience as an example, I hope to demonstrate that if Tanzania accepts the challenge of achieving a society in which women and men are equal, it is imperative that mechanisms are created to ensure that the relevant policies and laws are implemented. Parallel activities geared to bridge the gap between theory and practice will be needed. Without them laws enacted to promote equality are bound to seem empty or mere token commitments designed to appear to support equality while in fact bearing little relationship to what is happening at the practical level. The law, in other words, will remain a dead letter, and political speeches will only be platform platitudes paying lip-service to equality. There is also the danger that the existing laws and policies for promoting equality could be misused by the reactionary element within the state apparatus.

It is clear that women need to re-examine their role within society and endeavour, whenever opportunities present themselves, to take advantage of laws formulated in their favour, using them to further their long-term interests. The existing egalitarian laws and policies, though inadequate, have transformatory potential in that they provide a unique opportunity for women to challenge the remnants of negative traditions and customs. Failure to do so may lead to situations in which laws and policies enacted for the benefit of women might again be misused or misinterpreted by the predominantly male-dominated instruments of policy and law execution. The law itself may appear neutral, but the human actors who have to put it into practice might not be.

The women's organisations have an important role to play here in enlightening women on their rights because if women do not know the law, they will not have recourse to it. But even when they possess this knowledge and are committed to defending their rights, they need economic, social and institutional support to enable them to deal with instruments of the law with which they are unfamiliar and also in order to survive economically.

I was dismissed from my job in February 1985 as a consequence of the Tanzanian Government's directive to all its ministries, departments and parastatals to reduce operational costs. At the time of my dismissal, I was the Manpower Development and Administrative Manager of a government-owned company with which I had been working for ten years. I was the only woman manager in the company and also the only manager to be dismissed under the redundancy arrangements.

The order to institute redundancy was one of the Government's efforts to deal with the country's worsening economic position. When the Tanzanian Government had been forced to seek external aid, from the International Bank for Reconstruction and Development (IBRD), the World Bank and the IMF, it was required to observe and honour certain conditions. One of the conditions for securing appropriate loans, the Tanzanian Government was advised by its prospective creditors, was to seek means of reducing government spending and increasing efficiency in all government departments and parastatals.

Among the measures designed to meet the IBRD and IMF conditions were the steps taken to cut down labour costs by reducing the number of employees and to rationalise organisational structures. The Government issued a directive instructing immediate implementation of these measures. The government directive on cost-reduction was received with a mixed reaction by those who had to carry it out. Some regarded cost reduction by reducing the number of employees as unnecessary because their organisations were still expanding and also because they saw that such a step would create great hardship for the people who would be affected. Hence, they adopted a cautious approach to reductions in the workforce. Others responded zealously, seeing in this directive a golden opportunity to settle old scores, real or imagined, against colleagues or subordinates. Thus they completely disregarded the Government's rules and procedures regarding redundancy and terminated the services of many employees who should have remained at work. The third group of implementors veered between these two extreme positions.

In the ensuing exercise, about 15,000 employees were declared redundant. Most were women and men from middle and lower grades. As will become clear, the context in which the policy is made, and the relative power between individual members, even members of the same class, may during implementation influence the outcome of the said policy. The policy, which might at its inception appear to be neutral, may have an unpredictable outcome in a particular set of relations. In other words, there is a gap between policy at the theoretical level and its outcome in practice. This is because, as was pointed out earlier, decisions are continually being made at the implementation stage. For example, many top executives practised a lopsided kind of patriotism. When it came to making sacrifices in the national interest, not one of them was willing to offer himself/herself as a sacrificial lamb. They would offer only to remove those less powerful than themselves. Their greater relative power due to their greater proximity to the owner – the state – meant that some of these senior executives could, and did whenever they were allowed to get away with it, victimise individual employees under the pretence of acting in the national interest. They were, of course, acting in their own interest. Examples of victimisation appeared in many publicly owned institutions, including cases in which legal action was not taken.

My case, however, had another dimension: in it the interests of capital and of patriarchy converged, the one bolstering and reinforcing the other. The interests of capital dictated that the number of workers be cut down so that the production of wealth might continue unabated at minimum cost, while the interests of patriarchy dictated that it would be I who lost my job. Being female, I was seen not objectively, as a manager having rights and responsibilities, but subjectively, as a woman. The fact that I was head of my own household, in an economic environment where even two parental incomes were barely adequate to provide decent nutrition, and that I held the right qualifications and experience, was insufficient to deter my employers from declaring me redundant when it came to a choice between retaining me or an under-qualified junior who was a man. In my employers' eyes, as a woman I was not a breadwinner, though in my case my salary was not just a matter of buying cake but an issue of life and death for me and my family. Almost 20 years after the discourse on equality, social justice and human dignity came on to the Tanzanian political agenda, my employers still perceived me as a second-class citizen.

My analysis of my own situation and that of other women as members of the state bureaucracy is that we are bureaucrats with a difference. We may enjoy the same income as male bureaucrats, hold similar qualifications, adopt the same lifestyle, take our place on decision-making bodies, occupy an important position in the production process and enjoy control and proximity to the state apparatus; it is not unfounded to say, however, that we are perceived as belonging to an inferior gender. And this affects what we can or cannot achieve, as events in this case will reveal.

The other aspect of the case study is what may be called a 'hidden agenda' which constitutes part of the invisible but real reason why I was dismissed. Ultimately my dismissal had nothing to do with cost reduction or the national interest, which none the less formed an effective smoke screen. The real reasons arose in part from a set of attitudes, beliefs and opinions about what a 'good' woman should be. This also extends to what constitutes a 'good' woman manager and a 'good' wife. As will become clear by the end of the story, the contents of this agenda went beyond the confines of my home and my office; in fact the male formal and informal network succeeded in making it national if not international. By definition, I was not a 'good woman' and this reputation preceded or followed me wherever I went.

In 1984 my marriage broke down. I moved out of my husband's house into a company house. For reasons best known to my employers they decided to take sides and act in favour of my husband. My interpretation of this bias is that my action was seen as a challenge to the established patriarchal values which could set a bad precedent. Steps had to be taken to punish me as a deterrent to other women whose marriages had become intolerable to them. One of these steps was to order my eviction from the company house with seven days' notice on the grounds that my husband had complained. My continued occupation of the company house, my employers said, depended upon my getting a divorce decree or a letter from my husband giving his consent to my living separately from him. This demand was made in contravention of the laws and government directives in Tanzania that accord equal rights and privileges to both women and men. As a woman I was not seen to be an individual with legal and contractual rights. I was being defined as a wife in a situation that did not warrant such a definition. My marital status had not been one of the requirements for the job; it could not therefore become the basis for my being deprived of my employment rights. If people's private lives and conduct were to become part of the requirements for holding office, how many male bureaucrats would qualify to remain in the positions they now hold? Or is it simply a question of double standards; what's good for the goose is not good for the gander?

When I decided to prosecute my employers my aim was to challenge the hidden agenda, knowing as I did that such notions deriving from a patriarchal world view would not stand up to rigorous cross-examination in a court of law. I may have lacked alliances, a godfather and an informal network, but the law was still there to protect me. It was my only recourse. Now I could fully appreciate the importance of statutory legal rights. It took almost two years for my case to be concluded but in the end I was reinstated without loss of benefits.

One major lesson I learnt was that what we normally call the 'system' is composed of individuals whose values, attitudes and ideals are by no means homogeneous. The fact that I could get justice in the end through male-dominated structures showed me that there are some men with consciences who are committed to the principles of equality, fairness and justice and who see people as individuals and not as members of a particular gender. Such men act as moral pillars of strength in a potentially precarious and dangerous situation.

My case had a good deal of coverage in the Tanzanian media, another male-dominated institution which showed great sympathy to my case; and it evoked great interest from men and women alike. It was also quoted by the BBC as a classic example of the shameful waste of highly skilled manpower in a Third World country. Many people did not hold out much hope for my success because they believed that my dismissal had, in the first place, been sanctioned by the Government. What they failed to understand was the distinction between the legitimate objectives of the government directive on cost-cutting and the subjective manner of its implementation.

Part One introduces me to the reader, describing my educational and working background as well as the influences that shaped my feminist consciousness. It describes in detail the events that led to my dismissal and the reasons why I thought my case was based on victimisation and discrimination rather than on cost-reduction considerations. Part Two discusses the litigation, its hearing and the subsequent judgment. It gives a case calendar, and also touches briefly on other organisations or persons whom I approached in an effort to get an early solution to my case. Part Three discusses the events subsequent to the judgment. It shows the weaknesses in the laws governing industrial relations as well as pointing out deficiencies in the mode of accountability. Part Four draws conclusions and recommendations from the case history.

My hope is that this book will be of interest not only to women and workers but also to academics and practitioners in labour law as well as laypeople and those interested in human rights. I intend it to stimulate discussion, generate criticism and perhaps contribute to the gender-centred debate. Although my story is set in Tanzania, it is my hope that some of the issues raised will find echoes in other parts of the world.

PART ONE

The background

1

On 20 February 1985 at about 8.30 a.m. the General Manager of Fibreboards (Africa) Limited (FAL) summoned me to his office. He handed me a letter which he told me to read. Its contents were as follows:

> *Re: Post – Abolished*
>
> Reference is made to TWICO's letter Ref. No. WC/S of 9th February 1985.
>
> We are sorry to inform you that your post of Manpower Development and Administrative Manager has been abolished with effect from 20th February 1985 following the Government Directive to reduce costs and improve efficiency.
>
> You will be paid all your dues according to Government Directive. You are given seven days to vacate the company house from this date. You are not allowed to come to the factory premises unless you follow the laid down company procedures.

The letter was signed by the General Manager of FAL. A copy went to the General Manager of the Tanzania Wood Industry Corporation (TWICO) and a copy was to be lodged in my file. I was not surprised to receive this letter which only confirmed my long-held conviction that I would be dismissed at the least excuse.

I reflected on the letter's weaknesses. It struck me as odd for four reasons. First, it seemed to imply that not only was a post being abolished but that the functions I was employed to perform were also being done away with. In other words, post was being equated with function. My understanding was that it is possible to abolish or change a post's title without affecting its functions. Second, though the letter said that I was to be paid my dues according to government directive, it did not specify which government directive would apply. Third, though the letter seemed to imply that my services were being terminated, the total impact of its contents gave an entirely different picture. In fact my understanding was that I was being dismissed, since the contents of the letter did not seem to recognise the provisions of the company regulations that stipulated three months notice of dismissal or three months pay in lieu of notice. Since I was being removed purportedly in the national interest, it appeared remarkable and curious that these rights were being waived. Finally it struck me as extraordinary that I would not be allowed to enter company premises. All of a sudden I had become an enemy of the company. After ten years' service in positions of trust and responsibility, I was being discharged without honour and henceforth would come to the company premises as a stranger.

Paradoxically it was this letter which was to provide me with the ammunition I needed to fight for reinstatement. The General Manager and his henchmen had not prepared themselves adequately and the letter was going to prove their undoing. Before I go into the reasons why I hoped I would successfully challenge my employers, let me introduce the company and myself.

Fibreboards (Africa) Limited is a company that was legally instituted by Act of Parliament in 1972. Its main line of business is the manufacture of all types of wood-based products. It has a board of directors composed of government representatives, the Government being the sole shareholder, and other directors representing private lending institutions such as the Tanzania Investment Bank and the East African Development Bank. FAL is one of eleven subsidiaries of the Tanzania Wood Industry Corporation. TWICO, the holding company, was established by Act of Parliament in 1974 and was charged with the task of co-ordinating the activities of all the timber manufacturing companies owned by the Government in Tanzania. It has its own separate board of directors. FAL, however, is not a branch of TWICO, as evidenced by the fact that it has a legally autonomous board of directors which is entrusted with full powers to approve the company's budgets, make decisions on investment policies and deal with recruitment, promotion and the dismissal of the managerial grades. There is nothing in the Acts establishing FAL or TWICO that states categorically that the decisions of TWICO or of its board of directors would supersede or override decisions made by the board of directors of FAL. As such the role of TWICO is more that of overseer than of manager.

At the time of my dismissal, FAL had seven departments each headed by a manager, and I was head of the Manpower Development and Administration Department. As a consequence of the government directive to reduce costs, the organisational structure had to be rationalised from seven to four departments. The old structure is represented by diagram in Figure 1 (overleaf). What happened as a consequence of rationalisation is depicted in Figure 2. Three departments – Production (woodworking), Production (hardboard mill) and Maintenance – were merged to form the Processing Department. The Marketing Department and the Logging Department were left as before. The Finance Department and the Manpower Development and Administration Department, however, were combined to form the Finance and Administration Department.

Like other state-owned companies in Tanzania, FAL is subject to directives from several government bodies. The Ministry of Natural Resources and Tourism is the parent ministry and issues directives to all corporations and companies under its command. FAL has also to conform to the regulations laid down by the Presidential Standing Committee on Parastatal Organisations (SCOPO). (A parastatal is defined as a company in which the Government is the major or the sole shareholder, but which, due to the nature of its economic activities, does not come under direct ministerial control, thus enjoying some measure of quasi autonomy. Most Tanzanian parastatals carry out production, commerce or service activities.)

SCOPO was instituted to streamline the terms and conditions of service in the parastatal sector after Tanzania nationalised the commanding heights of the economy in 1967. There are more than 400 parastatals in Tanzania. FAL, like every other public institution, is subject to control from various other legally established government watchdogs. The Tanzanian Audit Corporation, for example, is a government corporation designed to audit the finances of the parastatals. In addition, parastatals are subject to the directives emanating from the President's Office, the Prime Minister's Office, the Ministry of Labour and Manpower, the Ministry of Economic Development and Planning, the Treasury, the Bank of Tanzania and last but not least the Ministry of Home Affairs. The various bodies to which FAL relates as an organisation are depicted in Figure 3 (overleaf).

In common with all parastatals, FAL is subject to laws governing industrial relations. These include the Security of Employment Act of 1964, which covers laws on redundancy and the establishment of Workers' Committees, and the Permanent Labour Tribunal Act of 1967, administered by the Permanent Labour Tribunal, one of whose functions is to adjudicate on trade dispute cases referred to

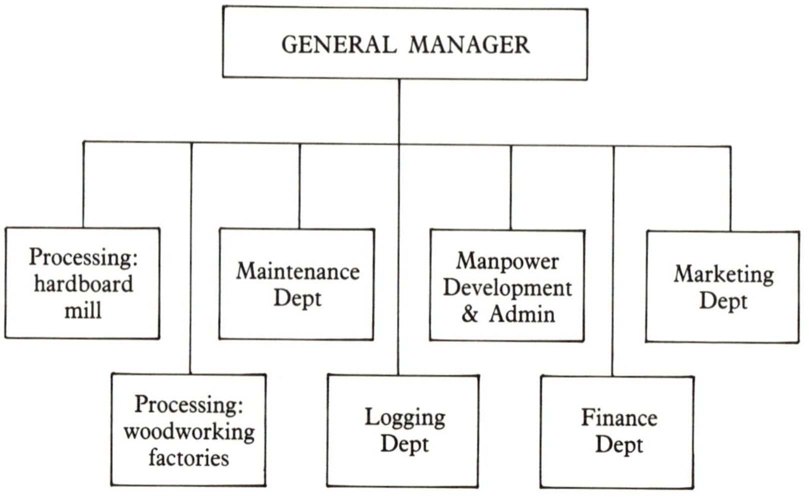

Figure 1
FAL organisational structure before rationalisation

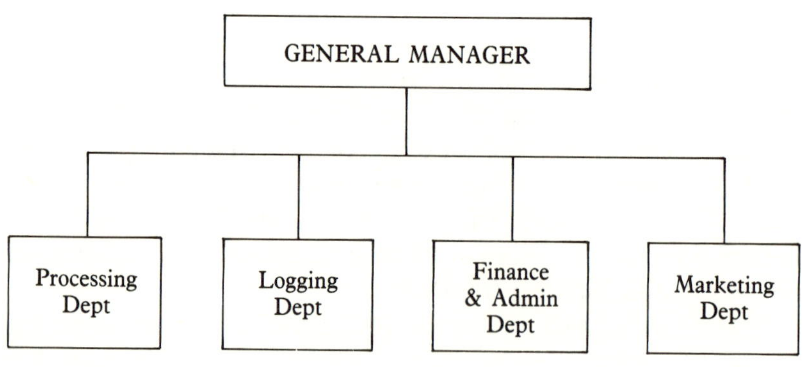

Figure 2
FAL organisational structure after rationalisation

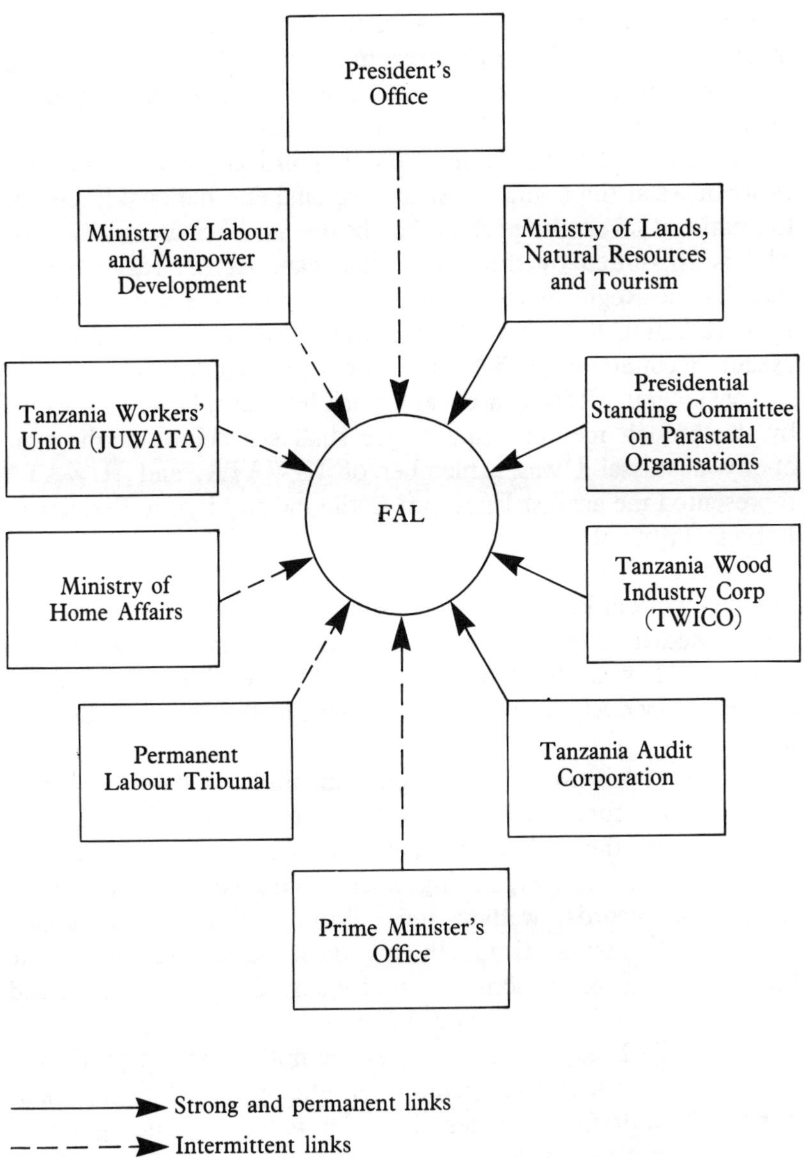

Figure 3
Offices, Ministries, Companies and other institutions from which FAL may receive directives

it by either the Minister of Labour or the Labour Commissioner in order to assess evidence and arrive at conclusions of fact or law.

Tanzania has only one workers' union, JUWATA, and its origins, structure and affiliation are similar to those of unions in other Third World countries. Every worker or manager is entitled to be a member. This is quite different from the situation in industrialised countries such as Britain where several unions may represent diverse groups. JUWATA in turn is affiliated to the Chama cha Mapinduzi (CCM), the ruling and only political party in Tanzania. It organises at the branch, district, regional and national levels. At the national level, the prime office bearer is the Secretary General who is appointed by the Party Chairman. At the regional level there is the Regional Union Secretary, and at the district level a District Union Secretary. All these officers are appointed by the executive council of JUWATA on the recommendation of the Secretary General. Office bearers at branch level are, however, elected by the branch membership. As we shall see below, at the time of my dismissal I was a member of JUWATA, and JUWATA represented me against FAL during the inquiry by the Permanent Labour Tribunal.

I started work at FAL as an Administrative Officer in August 1976. My immediate supervisor was the Personnel and Administrative Manager. He was educated to Standard Twelve (O level equivalent) and had previously been an army captain in the country's defence forces.

At FAL at this time there was only one mill, the hardboard mill, and a labour force of less than 100 employees. Initially I was charged with the task of reorganising the registry, supervising the secretarial staff, organising workers' transport, dealing with employees' records, welfare and cultural activities and making travel arrangements. Gradually my duties expanded to include certain aspects of personnel management due to the increased workload of the Personnel and Administrative Manager.

In 1978 FAL expanded from a single-mill operation producing hardboards to a four-mill operation producing sawn timber, woodwork and impregnated poles. In order to get a better grasp of personnel matters, I began to familiarise myself with certain important aspects, for example, the Security of Employment Act of 1964 which enabled me to know how to deal with employee infringement of rules and regulations. I studied the SCOPO rules, regulations and terms and conditions of service. I read FAL's Memoranda of Association in order to understand more fully what type of business we were in, what we planned to do, what the powers of the Board of Directors were, and so on.

My relationships with my subordinates were good and cordial even though there was a wide gap between the level of my education and theirs. The best educated were Standard Seven (top class in primary school) leavers. I felt that I commanded respect for my knowledge and authority and because I was the first woman university graduate the company had employed. The only other graduate in the company was a man. If I had any problems it was with the JUWATA officials: the Branch Chairman at the time felt it was beneath his dignity to deal with a woman. If there was an issue to be attended to, even if the matter was urgent, he used to wait until the Personnel Manager was free, rather than come to my office and see whether I could help. After some time I requested and was granted permission to be in attendance when Union officials were holding meetings with the Personnel Manager in order to gain some knowledge and experience in dealing with unions.

In the same year I was promoted to Personnel and Training Officer, with a considerable increase in salary. The General Manager, an Indian expatriate, congratulated me on my 'grand achievement' and earnestly hoped that I would continue to discharge my duties 'diligently in the best interests of the company and the nation'. I felt at the same time happy and somewhat fearful to have been given this promotion. I was happy because I felt recognised and appreciated: it was a confirmation that my efforts had not gone unnoticed. I was petrified, however, because I was not yet familiar with the training functions that my new job entailed – an aspect for which my first degree and my work experience had not equipped me. I decided that the best thing was to request further training and in my letter of acceptance of the new post I brought this to the General Manager's attention. He accepted my need for training in principle and promised to see that I got it. The opportunity presented itself the following year.

In October 1979 I left Tanzania for Britain to undertake a 15-month postgraduate diploma course in Personnel Management at Manchester Polytechnic. This was made possible by the British Technical Assistance Award which was and still is administered by the British Council in Tanzania. Prior to my departure for Britain, FAL appointed the man who would take over the post of Administrative Officer which had become vacant as a result of my being promoted. I had some reservations about his manner of recruitment and his qualifications. The job specification stipulated a BA degree in Administration. This particular man had Standard Eight education (the earlier top primary grade), had trained as a policeman and had worked as a security officer in the now defunct East African Community. I did not find my position appealing, sandwiched between this man and the Personnel and Administrative Manager, both individuals with military backgrounds. However, doing anything about it was beyond my power.

What I remember most about my early days in Manchester is its dismal weather. At first the weather and isolation affected me so badly that I feared I would be unable to complete the course successfully. As the lectures became more interesting, however, I became completely engrossed in trying to understand the British system of government, its history and institutions, which created the context of most of my study. The course was a multi-disciplinary one, very intensive and needing great effort on the part of the students. My own special interests were labour law, industrial relations and manpower training and development.

It was in Manchester that my perspectives altered and my consciousness of women's issues began to develop. I started to look for possibilities for social change that would affect the lives of women. In my study of industrial relations I found that women were grouped together with other 'disadvantaged' groups such as the disabled and children. I learnt that British women had problems trying to organise alone as women workers or within the male-dominated unions because the unions used the family ideologies to keep women subordinate even within the working environment. I also learnt that women had difficulties in organising alone as women because of their ambivalence towards work, which some saw as a stop-gap between school and marriage, and also because of the constraints imposed by the double burden of responsibilities at home and at the office or factory. I found, too, that women suffered from fragmented consciousness because of this ambivalence.

My interest aroused, I began to look at the position in Britain of women in senior posts in government or private institutions. Apart from Margaret Thatcher, there seemed to be very few prominent women in top positions. I began to explore the subject of women in management, to discover if there were specific problems encountered by women managers. Negative perceptions of women's ability to take on managerial positions were almost universal. The stereotype of women as passive, less competent and lacking in attributes deemed 'managerial' (competitiveness, drive, ambition, aggression) served to disqualify women from participating in an area seen as essentially a male preserve.

At the end of the course in 1981 I came away with a report

which said that I was an exceptional and impressive student, and had established very good results in areas requiring considerable knowledge of British institutions, knowledge which for a British student is mostly assumed. This report was sent to TWICO and is lodged in my personal file. On my return to Tanzania I received a letter of congratulations from the TWICO Training Manager on behalf of the General Manager of TWICO. I did not receive any formal recognition from FAL.

My lecturers at Manchester Polytechnic had warned us about the problem of trying to 'fit' back into the organisation after this kind of training. They had emphasised a tactful cautious approach but nothing in their instructions had prepared me adequately for what I actually experienced on my return to FAL.

The previous General Manager, the Indian expatriate, had completed his contract and left the country and the company was now headed by the former army captain who was also the Personnel Manager. He was my immediate boss. My immediate subordinate was the Administrative Officer who had trained as a policeman. Needless to say, exceptional skill was required to co-exist with two individuals whose managerial culture was so very different from mine. As far as I understand it, army culture is authoritarian, unidirectional and employs top-down commands. It is certainly not geared to accommodating consensus or democratic decision-making, for instance in an area like worker participation.

The new knowledge I had gained from my studies helped me to see what was happening in a different perspective. For example, Maslow's and Herzberg's theory of motivation taught me that the company had to design all types of incentives, monetary as well as non-monetary, to get the best out of its workers. One of the non-monetary incentives was to increase workers' participation in management so that the workers have some say in decisions about production and matters of their own welfare. Luckily, in my situation, this was supported by a presidential directive. Presidential Circular No. 1 (1970) required employers to run the state-owned enterprises in a democratic way. As the Training Officer for my firm I tried to get the management to implement this directive. I succeeded in getting the Workers' Council elected, but meetings were held only very rarely.

My relationship with JUWATA, on the other hand, improved. There was a new Chairman, but I felt that it was my added knowledge that gave me the advantage. I felt confident that now I could deal with the Union in a more congenial and conducive atmosphere. As a Training Manager, I arranged training sessions for Union officials on how to negotiate with the employer, how to prepare a defence for an employee facing a dismissal charge, and how to make timely interventions to represent workers' concerns. I was now in a better position to understand men's attitude towards women in managerial positions and know how to deal with it. I decided that it was best to let people know as early as possible where I stood, and having made a decision, to stand by it.

2

In June 1982, I became Manpower Development and Administrative Manager at FAL. By current standards, at thirty years of age, I was one of the youngest female managers in Tanzania. I believed I was headed for an even brighter future. In outline my new responsibilities were as follows:

- formulation of personnel policies
- direction and supervision of efficient secretarial services
- ensuring that rules and regulations were observed
- administration of recruitment matters
- periodic reviews of employee performance
- administration of training and manpower development matters
- supervision of the administration of employee benefits
- dealing with industrial grievances
- monitoring working and sanitary conditions
- public relations
- ensuring the security of company assets
- advising the General Manager on all personnel and administrative matters

My role at FAL now encompassed the activities of the entire organisation and was not limited to my own department. The personnel function, for instance, is both a line and a staff function. As a line manager I was responsible for my own departmental subordinates' performances. I had to ensure an efficient management of the day-to-day operations and development programmes of my department within the framework of the entire organisation development programme. In addition, I had to take an active part in the practical on-the-job training of the staff permanently or temporarily assigned to work in the department. Preparing the annual performance report and recommending promotion or salary increments for all the staff in my department was also part of my line function.

My staff functions, which in this case were advisory as well as executive, arose out of the nature of the functions that the Personnel Department had to perform for the company as a whole. For example, in administering recruitment matters, no head of department could do his own recruitment. According to my job description, not only did I arrange, conduct and participate in interviews of all personnel, I could also recommend or refuse to recommend a candidate to the recruiting department. As far as industrial relations were concerned, no head of department could dismiss an employee without the involvement of the Personnel Department.

As head of the Personnel Department, too, I was in charge of the open and confidential registry, and as such I had access to privileged information about all categories of employees, something not ordinarily enjoyed by other heads of departments. My staff and line functions also included ensuring observation of company rules and regulations; administering wage and salary policies as well as the grading of workers; supervising procedures to ensure periodic reviews of employee performance; supervising the administration of employee benefit entitlements such as leave, health, housing, workmen's compensation and others.

As far as training and manpower development were concerned, I was responsible for initiating and supervising the establishment of training and other programmes, for eliciting the co-operation of the line managers to determine training priorities, and for developing the full range of training programmes best geared to solve specific problems facing the organisation. I was also charged with ensuring that the established manpower development programmes were fully implemented, and also that there was full workers' participation in management programmes. In the area of staff appraisal, it was my duty to collect the performance evaluation reports from the heads of departments, add my own comments and prepare promotion proposals for presentation to management.

The Personnel and Administration Department was a powerful one. By virtue of my position and according to the company finance regulations, I was one of the FAL bank signatories (together with the General Manager and Chief Accountant) empowered to approve expenditure up to Tsh.10,000, a power that I rarely exercised thanks to the informal withdrawal of that power by the General Manager. I also attended the company Board meetings as an observer, or in case I was required to clarify certain personnel and administrative matters.

The influence enjoyed by me as the head of this powerful department is an important factor in understanding my dismissal. The decisions that I made at certain times – or those which I had to oppose – in pursuit of what I believed to be reasonable, fair and just were not always seen in that light. And the fact that the head of this powerful department was a woman added, in my view, another dimension. I had the impression that the other departmental heads, all men, had difficulty consulting me when the decisions I had to make related to their departments. They had no choice, however, but to abide by the established procedures, which required that my department be involved in all matters of personnel and administration. The extent of their ill-feeling was clearly demonstrated when none of them came to commiserate with me on my dismissal as would have been customary.

When I became head of the Manpower and Administration Department, I started reorganising it and giving it a new image. I was specifically concerned with establishing a sense of security in workers' employment as I wanted the workers to feel confident that the principles of fairness and justice would prevail above everything else. I had a small booklet printed that told the workers not only of their rights but also what the company expected of them. I set about redesigning the format for staff evaluation reports to include sections whereby workers would participate in their own evaluation. Previously all staff appraisal reports were the prerogative of the supervisors and heads of departments and were confidential. In order to get the heads of departments to use the new format we had a meeting in which I explained and extolled the virtues of involving the workers in their own evaluation. The format was accepted and used. In fulfilling my training functions I set about changing the way the company identified training needs. Previous training had been carried out, I felt, without due regard to the organisation's objective of meeting employees' own needs. In making these changes I sought support from my colleagues.

Their reaction was a mixed one. Some were very supportive, some were not; a few were hostile. But we got on. I accepted conflict and disagreement as part and parcel of my organisational life. However, as we shall see, some of these conflicts contributed further to my dismissal.

One particular area of conflict concerned the use of company cars. The company cars were normally pooled with the Administration Department, from which other departments requested their use for various company activities. However, the General Manager could remove any company car without notice and without letting anyone in my department know that a certain car was now being sent on an errand. However, when I approached the General Man-sent on an errand. However, when I approached the General Manager and pointed out that personal activities should not interfere with the smooth functioning of organisational activities, the company cars were removed from the Administration Department and allocated to other departments. I shall come back to this aspect later.

Other types of conflict were more covert and indirect. From time to time at management team meetings, I had a sense that I was being upstaged by the other members in the way they would sometimes use a language I could not understand or in the way the agenda was skimmed through, leaving me with a feeling that the issues had been decided on before the meeting was formally convened. There did not seem to be as much spontaneous and thorough discussion of issues as might have been expected. At times I felt very isolated and alone.

There were two areas where I firmly put my foot down and refused to be swayed by others; these were in respect of the recruitment and dismissal of employees. I always made sure that recruitment was based on merit, and I was strictly against nepotism. As far as dismissals were concerned, I normally insisted on very strict proof of any offence alleged by heads of departments, supervisors or foremen. If the head of department could not provide sufficient grounds for dismissal, my department would normally refuse to fulfil his recommendations. In order to protect my own standing and credibility in case the aggrieved employee took his or her case before the Labour Tribunal or Conciliation Board I had to be very sure of the facts. It was my conviction that being a female or male personnel manager did not matter when it came to such questions. To me, a personnel manager who stands before a Tribunal or Conciliation Board and fails to substantiate the reasons for dismissal makes a mockery of the profession.

Another area of disagreement concerned standing in for the General Manager. It was customary at FAL, when the substantive post holder went away on company business, for the Manpower Development and Administrative Manager to take the position of Acting General Manager. When I became the Manpower Development and Administrative Manager at FAL, the General Manager completely abandoned this practice so that either the Chief Accountant or Production Manager became Acting General Manager. I had a feeling that this was done not because I was incompetent but because I was a woman. It was only when some problem arose in the General Manager's absence and the Acting General Managers found it difficult to decide on certain issues that they turned to me, perhaps reluctantly, for advice. Thus it was that on one such occasion I came into direct confrontation with the General Manager of TWICO. He had come to FAL ostensibly on a mission to supervise personally the eviction of a Tanzanian engineer from a company house in order to install a Finnish expert who had been recruited to work at FAL. The Chief Accountant who was FAL's Acting General Manager at the time called me for advice. My advice both to the General Manager of TWICO and to the Chief Accountant was against evicting the Tanzanian engineer, whom I said would feel degraded and demoralised. I thought that the local engineer might be led to resign if he was removed in preference to another person and this would constitute constructive dismissal on the part of the employer. In my opinion, acquisition of foreign expertise could not be undertaken at the risk of demoralising local experts. After all, since independence it has been one of Tanzania's development objectives to be self-sufficient in manpower. Thus I advised against evicting the local engineer and, instead, recommended that the company accelerate its efforts in looking for alternative accommodation for the foreign expert. This answer obviously displeased the General Manager of TWICO who said that I was not fit to be a Personnel Manager.

I had another confrontation with the TWICO General Manager over Management's recommendation to dismiss an officer for his failure to purchase nuts and bolts, which had cost the company an entire day's production of hardboards. This issue was taken before the Board of Directors, whose Chairman was the General Manager of TWICO. I was assigned the task of presenting the motion for dismissal before the Board. At the conclusion of my presentation, the TWICO General Manager attacked me on the manner of my presentation which in any case, he said, did not prove that the officer had been negligent. My reply was that the fact that there was no production on the day in question due to lack of nuts and bolts proved negligence. I further pointed out that the Production Department had also advanced this as a reason for their failure to turn out any goods. Nevertheless, the officer was reinstated and thereafter made no bones about seeing me as his enemy. I later learnt that the General Manager of TWICO and the officer in question came from the same village and were actually close neighbours.

Outside FAL I was making connections which ensured that my personal development was not limited to the firm I worked for. In 1982 I was elected to become the first woman member of the

(ATE). In this capacity I was able to represent the Association in international and national meetings. For example, in 1984 I represented the Association as an observer at a meeting on planning organised by the Ministry of Economic Development and Planning to discuss measures to deal with the economic crisis. In 1983 and 1984, I attended two other meetings, in Arusha and Nairobi, of the Association of Employers from English-speaking Countries. I learnt much from these meetings, not only in terms of the subject matter but also in terms of public speaking.

In relation to issues regarding the interests of women I began to see my participation in such meetings as providing me with a unique opportunity to raise questions relating to women's concerns. In 1984, at a SCOPO symposium for personnel managers, I volunteered to present a paper under that year's theme of 'Workers' Participation in Management'. My paper was entitled 'The Factors Inhibiting the Participation of Women in Decision Making at Senior Level in the Government and Parastatal Organisations'. In it I pointed out that, even though women were part of the labour force, and thus theoretically eligible to be elected to participate in the vehicles of workers' participation (the Workers' Councils), there were social and cultural factors inhibiting their participation. I argued that the two most important factors were stereotyping and educational background. Stereotyping acts in such a way that even should a woman be well enough educated, she would still be perceived as being unable to perform managerial work: traditional attitudes saw women as unable to command and direct others. The educational background was a factor because few women in Tanzania were highly qualified due to lack of access to further education or unsuitable specialisation with regard to managerial skills. Furthermore, since most women were not heads of institutions or departments they could not enjoy automatic admission into the Workers' Councils.

I looked at the recruitment and selection of candidates to senior positions and pointed out that this was biased against women in the sense that even if female candidates applied, rarely did they get shortlisted to attend an interview. When shortlisted, they were more often than not forced to face an exclusively male interviewing panel which had no sympathy with female candidates. Once past the appointment hurdle, in terms of work assignments, it happened that women would not be given those jobs that were commensurate with their abilities, but rather jobs that employers thought were suitable for females. I recommended that women should be assigned duties that *did* match their true abilities. Furthermore, I argued that personnel managers did not give equal consideration to women in terms of training and promotion opportunities and that they tended to decide *for* women, instead of leaving them to make their own decisions. Women's inability to go for further training was assumed.

Finally, I pointed out that women lack female role models in senior positions and are further disadvantaged in not having access to the all-male informal network of contacts and mentors, 'the old-boy network', important for mobility within the organisation. Women's progress was further constrained by inappropriate demands from would-be mentors or the fear of being misunderstood by others if the mentor was of the opposite sex. The paper, which was later published, was well received by the predominantly male audience and actually made news on the national radio.

In 1983 I was invited by the African Training and Research Centre for Women of the Economic Commission of Africa (ECA) to participate in a methodological meeting in Addis Ababa on 'Women and Industrialisation' in which four countries, including Tanzania, were to be used as examples of how women would be integrated in industrialisation in line with the Lagos Plan of Action. Three other women, from Nigeria, the Ivory Coast and Egypt, contributed a chapter each to an ECA publication entitled *Women and the Industrial Development Decade in Africa*. My own chapter was titled 'Women, Socialism and the Basic Industrialisation Strategy'.

In 1982 and 1983 I was invited as a resource person to attend the East and Southern African Management Institute (ESAMI) for the course on 'Women in Development'. Again in 1983 I was a participant in a workshop for Senior Women Executives at ESAMI organised jointly by the Commonwealth Secretariat, ECA and ESAMI. In February 1984 I was elected by the Arusha Regional Conference of the Women's Organisation – the Tanzania Women's Union, Umoja wa Wanawake wa Tanzania – to be a member of the Women's Regional Executive Committee, and to represent the Women's Organisation at the Regional Party Conference. Needless to say, my feminist consciousness was strengthened by these multiple experiences. In 1984 I was invited by the United Nations Industrial Development Organisation (UNIDO) Training Branch, in Vienna, to participate in designing a modular curriculum for Training in Industrial Management for Women Entrepreneurs. This invitation was based on my experience as a woman manager in a developing country. In Vienna as well as in Addis Ababa I was exposed to women of international standing and reputation, experts in the field of women and development from whom I learnt much. It was fortunate that all my travelling coincided with my annual leaves.

3

I cannot pinpoint exactly when I began to perceive that matters were not going as smoothly as they should, but I would say that my problems with FAL began towards the end of 1983. What triggered the process, however, is less puzzling to me now that I look back. The principal reason seems to have been my demonstration of expertise on my return from Manchester which threatened the position and status of certain people in the organisation. The other reason was the fact that I had begun to be recognised both nationally and internationally. Additional factors, I believe, were my stubbornness in refusing to co-operate with and sanction what I saw as unethical practices and my outspokenness on certain issues. Finally it could be that my call for recognition of women's abilities with regard to appointments to senior positions was interpreted as a personal strategy to get recognition of my own abilities and this again was experienced by some people as threatening to their positions. It is very difficult, however, to demonstrate conclusively that this was the case. The facts I am about to narrate are the same facts that I later put before the Permanent Labour Tribunal to prove that I had been victimised.

Late in 1983 I began to observe certain practices on the part of the General Manager that I interpreted as calculated to discredit my performance, degrade me personally as a manager, and affect negatively my standing in the eyes of the labour force. His actions included, for example, reversing decisions after my department had made recommendations as to which employees would be laid off because of temporary closure of the plant for renovation purposes. These recommendations were made after scrutinising the employees' records and determining the company's requirements during renovation in terms of qualifications, and also by applying the 'First In, Last Out' principle whereby the longest-serving employees (First In) are the last to lose their jobs under the redundancy procedures. The FAL management team had together drawn up a list after which I had posted notices alerting the employees of the temporary closure and also detailing the names of the employees who would be affected. I notified JUWATA accordingly.

One week later FAL's General Manager, without consulting anyone from my department, called a workers' meeting while I was in town attending official business and completely reversed the agreed layoff procedure. Using criteria known only to himself he read out another list, different from the one that was already on the notice board. On my return, my office was swamped with questions from workers who felt they had been unfairly treated. I wrote to the General Manager to ascertain his reasons for changing the agreed procedure but he did not bother to reply. My feelings were that the workers treated this as a lack of a firm stand by my department over a very sensitive issue.

Secondly, it suddenly became the General Manager's habit to bypass me in favour of my subordinate, the Administrative Officer, who thus started to carry out functions within my department without my knowledge. This was not as simple as it might appear: because literally my subordinate became my *de facto* boss, giving me orders at the direction of the General Manager. This is how, for example, all the company vehicles previously in the common pool within the Administration Department were removed from my department without my knowledge and distributed among the other departments. My junior, the Administrative Officer, was directed to inform me of the General Manager's decision. This made it difficult for me to fulfil welfare functions such as attending to sick employees or their eligible relatives (wives, children, etc.). I wrote to the General Manager to bring this to his attention but he did not reply.

Conflicts came to a head in June 1984 when the head of the Finnish team attacked me without cause during a Production meeting. Tanzania, like many other Third World countries, is a recipient of aid from Finland: in this case the Finnish team, a firm called EKONO, were under an obligation to carry out renovations of all FAL mills and also to train local personnel according to what was called the Rationalisation Contract. As an officer in charge of the training function it was my responsibility to formulate an appropriate method for ensuring a transfer of skills from the Finnish experts to local personnel. In any case the requirement to train Tanzanians was the responsibility of every parastatal company according to Directives Nos. 10, 11 and 14 of SCOPO. The ultimate objective was to be self-sufficient in manpower. I believed the key words were 'systematic training', and I sought to change and redefine the way of assessing and evaluating training then in use. In an internal memo to the Finnish experts and to their local counterparts, I alerted them to the need to prepare a training plan. The purpose of the training plan would be to identify training objectives and training needs, designating appropriate methods of training, training implementation and ultimately training evaluation in the light of the original or supplementary objectives. I asked for co-operation from everyone in this matter.

Some of the local people wrote back to me to express their dissatisfaction with the way the transfer of skills between experts and local personnel was being implemented so far. They expressed optimism that the new system might help. The Finnish experts remained silent. Ultimately I took an opportunity during one of our meetings to broach the issue of my memo. There were eight people at the meeting: two Production Managers, the Maintenance Engineer, three Finnish personnel, the General Manager and myself. The Finnish Project Manager said that the method I proposed demanded too much work. I suggested that I could help in compiling the data with the individuals concerned, then went on to remind him that a 'systematic' transfer of skills was part of his duties in accordance with the SCOPO directives.

A fierce argument ensued between the Finnish Project Manager and myself. I maintained that as a training manager, I had to submit a report to the Board at the end of the Rationalisation Contract to demonstrate the extent of the skills acquired by Tanzanian nationals. I did not then know that such a report might never be requested. The Finnish Project Manager said he was not going to let his experts do paperwork as it was time-consuming. After a heated debate the Finnish Project Manager said that he would use his position to abolish my useless department and ensure my dismissal before he completed his contract.

I was astonished and, indeed, rendered speechless for a time. What had started as an objective argument had turned into a forum for personal attacks and threats. Through it all the General Manager made no intervention in his role as chairman of the meeting. I felt that I should not let the happenings of the day pass unrecorded. That same day I wrote to the General Manager repeating what the Finnish Project Manager had said and requesting him to clarify his position with regard to the Project Manager's words. I further enquired whether what had happened at that meeting was part of a conspiracy to frustrate and intimidate me, and to disrupt my effectiveness as head of the Personnel Department. I never received an answer to that letter.

Until now I have avoided talking about my domestic life. I am forced to mention it here because my domestic problems were dragged into my working environment by my husband and my employers. My private affairs became part of a 'hidden agenda' which was used most effectively by certain individuals strategically placed in senior positions to block my opportunities and chances.

It is a sad irony that in the office I was, at least in theory, powerful, yet at home I was powerless. In the office I could make decisions regarding people's livelihoods and communicate with those at the top and the bottom of the hierarchy. At home I felt uncertain, constantly aware that I could not make important decisions. Someone else decided for me, and I had to pretend that I was less knowledgeable, less capable.

In 1984, after ten years of marriage, I separated from my husband. Since I was living in my husband's employer's house I was forced to look for alternative accommodation. In accordance with SCOPO regulations, housing was one of my entitlements as a personnel manager. As such, I wrote to the General Manager, requesting a company house which had remained vacant for three months following the resignation of the company's Chief Accountant. It took another month, however, for the Housing Committee to convene and allocate me this house. In February 1984 I moved into my new home where I still live as I write this book.

Late in February 1984, as I was in the middle of presenting my paper on 'Factors Inhibiting the Participation of Women in Decision Making at Senior Level in the Government and Parastatal Organisations' I received a message that I was wanted at FAL. I reported to the General Manager who informed me that my husband had called at the company premises and had threatened to take the company to court allegedly for allocating me a separate house while I was still legally his wife. I was informed, moreover, that a Management meeting had been convened and that the team had insisted that the allocation of the company house was in accordance with my employment entitlement. The management team had accordingly advised my husband that he could move in with me if he liked; it was up to him to settle the matter with me. I felt that that was a fair reply.

Apparently, my husband did not go to court. He decided, rather, to appeal to the holding company, TWICO, and whatever he told the General Manager there had the desired effect. To this day I do not know what transpired between these two men. The General Manager of TWICO obviously did not consider it necessary to call me to get my side of the story. Below is part of the letter sent to the General Manager of FAL by the General Manager of TWICO, a photocopy of which I was given:

> **Re: Company House allocated to Mrs Mukurasi**
> We have recently been informed that FAL management did allocate a company house to Mrs Mukurasi, an employee of your company without written consent of her husband Mr Mukurasi . . .
>
> While we appreciate your company's humanitarian approach to your workers' problems, we do not however condone the steps taken by you in providing this lady with a company house *without the consent of her husband*. Mr Mukurasi has personally called to this office complaining about FAL's Housing Committee's move to allocate a house to his wife without his knowledge.
>
> *If these facts are correct* then it would appear that your housing committee was ill-informed or did misdirect itself in allocating Mrs Mukurasi a company house . . .
>
> After evaluating the matter we are now directing you to take the following steps immediately:
>
> Require Mrs Mukurasi to vacate the company house with immediate effect *unless she produces a letter from a court of law evidencing that she is a divorcee*. She should vacate the company house within seven days from the date of this letter.
>
> (*my emphasis*)

The letter was signed by the General Manager of TWICO.

I was dismayed that a senior officer of a public corporation could either display such ignorance, or dare to violate on such a scale his own country's laws, rules and regulations. An officer of his seniority ought to have known better. In the first instance, Tanzania had enacted a number of laws that are in principle meant to give equal rights to both men and women in employment. My housing and other entitlements came to me as part of my employment contract and did not depend on my marital status. Government Standing Order No. 20 and SCOPO Directive No. 44 made it clear that both men and women would receive similar treatment in terms of salary and fringe benefits. Moreover my position in the company and my salary grade provided sufficient grounds for such an entitlement. In any case, my marital status had not been one of the qualifications for the job. I had been employed on merit, on the basis of my academic record. I reasoned that the General Manager of TWICO was interpreting the laws to suit his own male chauvinist views based on the patriarchal values of male supremacy.

On the other hand by directing that I be removed from the company house the General Manager of TWICO might have been trying to force me to go back to my husband. I reasoned that if this was the case then he was contravening the provisions of the Marriage Act of 1971 which made it clear that even a court of law could not force a person to cohabit with their partner against his or her will. Furthermore, the General Manager of TWICO had contravened the principles of natural justice by failing to give me an audience before condemning me. His letter actually said: 'If these facts are correct', meaning that he was not interested in finding out the truth before acting. I doubted whether the General Manager of TWICO would have ordered my husband's eviction had our positions been reversed. It was being made clear that my usefulness to the company depended on my remaining married. Now that I needed all the help I could get, the General Manager of TWICO did not want to be embarrassed by being associated and identified with me. Like Pontius Pilate he washed his hands in public. I was to be thrown out of the company house and yet was still expected to perform my duties as a faithful Personnel Manager! I deduced that the TWICO General Manager wanted me to make a constructive decision. In other words, he did not care if I resigned, which amounted to constructive dismissal in law.

Thirdly, from my understanding his action was *ultra vires*: he had no legal power to reverse a decision made by FAL's Housing Committee in the matter of allocation of housing for their employees. What he ordered had only an intimidatory effect, rather than being in any sense legal. I decided that I was not going to be intimidated.

The FAL General Manager wrote a letter to me whose contents are reproduced below, enclosing the copy of the letter from TWICO's General Manager:

> I have been directed to inform you, that you should vacate the company house which you were allocated by FAL Housing Committee on 16th January 1984. You are given seven days to vacate the house from the date you receive this letter.
>
> We are sorry to say that we cannot shoulder the issue any more due to the pressure from your husband.

Like a good soldier the FAL General Manager was willing to be guided, right or wrong, by his commander. Later he would come to say, not unlike the officers during the famous Nuremberg Trials, that he was simply obeying his superior's orders.

As soon as I received this letter I wrote to the General Manager of FAL, calling attention to the three points set out above. I concluded my letter by stating that I did not consider the directives given by the General Manager of TWICO to be reasonable and lawful and that as such I was not bound to obey them. I sent copies of this letter to TWICO and SCOPO. I also wrote to the JUWATA branch at FAL drawing their attention to the letter from the General Manager of TWICO. JUWATA convened a meeting which was attended by both the General Manager of FAL and myself. The General Manager was told in no uncertain terms that by ordering me to vacate the company house he had implemented an unlawful order. JUWATA similarly condemned the action of TWICO's General Manager.

In my indignation at the injustice, I decided to take extra precautions. For the first time, I visited the solicitors who were to support me throughout my case, Messrs Mwale and Ojare, Advocates of Arusha Town. I requested that they file an application for an injunction restraining my employers from disturbing my peace.

Five days after receiving notice to vacate the company house, I managed to secure a temporary court injunction, subject to the condition that the matter would be further deliberated after the hearing of the main suit. That temporary injunction was actually very timely, as I am convinced it bailed me out of a very embarrassing situation. After the hearing of the main suit, this is what the magistrate decided, quoted verbatim.

> In view of what the plaintiff told this court and after a thorough reconnaissance of the documents tendered forth by the plaintiff, I am quite convinced that the act of the defendants is a result of undue influence of the plaintiff's husband whom they have separated. In the circumstances I enter judgment in favour of the plaintiff with the usual consequences. I declare the plaintiff a lawful occupant of house No. 130 Amani Road. She is entitled to the said house as a member of management team of Fibreboards (Africa) Ltd. and was legally allocated the said house by Fibreboards' Housing Committee. I further restrain the plaintiff's employer from disturbing her peaceful possession of the said house. Order accordingly. (Civil Case No. 30/84 Laeticia Mukurasi vs. Fibreboards (Africa) Limited and Tanzania Wood Industry.)

I was overjoyed to get this ruling which clearly confirmed the equality principle enshrined in both the standing orders and the government directives. I thought that I would be able to continue my work in peace. But I was wrong.

In June 1984 I began to get an inkling that forces were gathering to remove me from the company permanently. In that same month the following telex arrived at FAL:

> FAL
>
> Please advise effective working days spent outside your factory by your Manpower Development and Administrative Manager (MDAM), including number of days she was absent or on leave attending conferences in Dar es Salaam or doing research work not connected with FAL duties or any other unauthorised absences. We request this information for our record purposes.
>
> Regards
>
> TWICO

I blessed the day I found the telex. The contents surprised me but did not shock me. I knew now for sure that I would be made to pay for thwarting the eviction. Obviously I was heading for a showdown, and the TWICO General Manager was not going to waste any opportunity to flex his managerial muscles and show me who was the boss. He was trying to establish grounds for a summary dismissal. Feeling like a criminal hounded on all fronts, I began to make my way more cautiously.

The telex that was sent in reply ran as follows:

> Att. GM TWICO
>
> *Days Spent Outside the Factory by MDAM*
>
> Required by you the following days spent out by MDAM during 1983 and 1984:
>
> 1983
>
> | | |
> |---|---|
> | January | 5 days SCOPO seminar |
> | February | 1 day sick |
> | March | 4 days on official trip |
> | April | 1 day seminar |
> | May | 13 days seminar |
> | June | 3 days on official trip |

August	12 days on official trip
September	14 days on official trip
October	2 days on official trip
November	3 days pass out and 6 on official trip
December	2 days on official trip

1984	
January	16 days SCOPO seminar
February	24 days annual leave
March	4 days leave
May	8 days on official trip
June	10 days to attend funeral in Bukoba and 3 days sick leave.

What this amounted to was that my absences from the company had been legally sanctioned. The General Manager of TWICO could not on this basis formulate grounds to dismiss me. I suspected, however, that other means to remove me would be devised.

I did not have to wait long: soon subtle and not-so-subtle hints began to be given that I was going to be dismissed. In September 1984, for example, during a Housing Committee meeting, the Finnish Project Manager who was Acting General Manager wanted to know when I would vacate the company house in which I was living. I wondered why he was asking until he mentioned that TWICO was in the process of recruiting an administrative specialist for Fibreboards who would be head of the reconstituted Finance and Administration Department after the rationalisation of the company's organisational structure. The Finnish Project Manager further informed the committee that this new department would absorb the department I was heading as part of the cost-reduction measure. I replied that I would vacate the company house if I were to be legally dismissed from the company. Afterwards I wrote to the General Manager of TWICO through an intermediary enquiring about the matter. I did not receive a reply to this letter.

Reduction in the number of employees as a measure to deal with the national economic crisis was beginning to be contemplated by the Government. I reasoned that removing me for reasons of cost reduction would be problematic (and this is what it ultimately turned out to be). With my good service record, qualifications and seniority, I reasoned that no one in his right mind would think of removing me on cost-reduction considerations. I was wrong again.

On 24 January 1985 the General Manager of FAL convened a Management meeting to discuss how cost reduction was going to be implemented at FAL. JUWATA, the Union, was represented. As Personnel Manager, I explained that we had always strived to keep manning levels in line with production capability at all times. As such only half the labour force was currently in employment since the plants were producing at less than half capacity. My argument was supported by all the other managers and it was agreed finally that there would be no redundancies but that we would restrict expenditure by the following amounts:

Local and overseas travel to be reduced by	Tsh. 50,000
Staff welfare, uniforms and canteen	100,000
Recruitment, militia training, CCM and JUWATA	40,000
Motor vehicles maintenance	550,000
Office expenses	320,000
Total Tsh.	1,560,000

With that settled, I felt that maybe my fears concerning my job security were unfounded. The decision not to reduce the labour force was a Management decision that would get the blessing of the Board of Directors of FAL. Little did I suspect that the General Manager of TWICO would devise other 'legitimate' ways of getting rid of me permanently.

On the morning of 20 February 1985 I received my letter of dismissal.

My dismissal was not totally unexpected. I can say that I saw it coming although I did not know that the General Manager of TWICO would be so ruthless as to use a legitimate government directive in such a manner. What my employers did not realise was that my level of consciousness regarding women's oppression and subordination was such that not to oppose this act would have seemed like a betrayal, not only of myself, but of all women.

My knowledge of labour law and industrial relations and my experience as a personnel manager were certainly an advantage. It is inconceivable that, with the knowledge I possessed as a result of my academic background and my experience, I could have let my employer get away with this unfair act. According to labour legislation, redundancy may be considered an option when there is a cessation of business, or when there is a cessation or diminution of the requirements of the business for the work of a particular kind. As it turned out FAL dismissed only 29 employees out of 371, which did not constitute a significant diminution of the requirement for personnel work. On the other hand, if the functions of the Personnel Department were no longer required, then it was logical that the entire workforce in that department should have been dismissed as a measure to reduce costs. It seemed suspicious and absurd that the cost-reduction measures should affect only the head of the department.

In addition, I was aware that the employer had an obligation to consult with JUWATA in case of redundancy, and this applied to the entire labour force regardless of position. Section 6(1)g of the Security of Employment Act states:

> The function of the field branch, and in relation to the business for which it is established, is to consult with the employer concerning impending redundancies and the application of any joint agreement on redundancies.

We had agreed during the meeting on 24 January 1985 that there would not be any redundancies. No other consultative meeting was held with JUWATA before my dismissal. Perhaps my employers thought that the success of their act depended on the element of surprise. Consulting the Union would have let the cat out of the bag and, in my opinion, it is doubtful if JUWATA would have accepted my dismissal for cost-reduction purposes. To my employers I must have appeared to be such an easy target for victimisation. Without a job I was deprived of my economic independence, without a husband I was completely lacking in any kind of fall-back position. Without a house there would never be a fighting space. A combination of all these factors no doubt strengthened my employers' conviction that they could get away with this discriminatory act. They were wrong.

Furthermore, I recollected my labour law classes on the principle of 'First In, Last Out'. Since I had been at FAL for almost ten years, it appeared inconceivable that I should be dismissed before people who had been employed long after me. I deemed it unfair, for example, that I should be dismissed and yet the Administrative Officer, who was appointed much later than me, be left behind to carry out the functions I had previously performed. In addition I was aware that throughout TWICO and its subsidiaries, I was among the best-qualified personnel managers, both academically and in terms of experience. TWICO had blessed my going for further studies and had also acknowledged my achievements at the end of the course. My career advancement within the company had been very rapid. The company's Board of Directors had never given me a warning or a reprimand for any reason whatsoever. The ingredients for success and further advancement all appeared to be there.

The other grounds for contesting my dismissal were formulated after I received my letter of dismissal: the mode of implementing the government directive struck me as suspect. For example, two other heads of department who had had their departments abolished or merged with other departments in the reorganisation of the company's structure had been absorbed within the organisation. Logically they should have met the same fate as myself. Was it significant that both were men? Sex discrimination meant that I was not given the same chance. As far as I was concerned this was an extreme example of the glorification of the concept of the male breadwinner. My employers were aware that an income for me, in the circumstances prevailing then, was not a matter of luxury. I was head of my household and my life and that of my family members depended on it.

Most surprising, however, was that immediately after my dismissal, the company employed an Indian expatriate to head the newly constituted Finance and Administration Department. The remuneration paid to this expatriate amounted to eight times or more what I was earning. The question was, what was the element of cost reduction? It was later to be argued before the Tribunal that the expatriate's remuneration was met by EKONO, the Finnish firm carrying out a renovation project at FAL. However, as was argued by JUWATA before the same Tribunal, the same money paid to this expatriate could have been used to purchase spare parts for FAL mills. Alternatively, and this is my view, since the retirement age in Tanzania is 55, the company should have considered the possibility of sending me for further studies in finance management. I believed that my potential for further career development had been amply demonstrated. This to me seemed a much sounder investment as at the time in question, I still had, all things being equal, 20 years of working life left.

If, however, the argument was that I was earning a bigger salary in comparison to the Administrative Officer who was left to perform personnel duties, then by the same argument, the first person to have been dismissed or to have volunteered to be retrenched in the national interest should have been the General Manager. He was earning more than anyone else in the company.

Finally, the move to dismiss me, initiated by TWICO and not by FAL's Board of Directors, was in my view *ultra vires*; it was not legally tenable that I should be dismissed from TWICO. Since

I was legally employed by FAL, the General Manager of TWICO had no direct power to order my dismissal. He could only have possessed such a power had the FAL Board of Directors approved my dismissal. I was aware that the FAL Board of Directors had not convened to discuss cost reduction. The General Manager of FAL, on the other hand, by dismissing me without the Board of Directors' consent, had implemented an unlawful order.

Armed with these facts, I believed I could successfully challenge the actions of the General Managers of TWICO and FAL and their collaborators. I was convinced, too, that the question of my reinstatement was one of time, and I was willing to bide my time. The struggle now began in earnest.

PART TWO

Investigation and adjudication

4

I had made a deliberate and conscious decision to challenge my employers in order to get reinstated. Now I had to formulate a strategy towards this end.

My strategy had three parts. First I had to process my case according to the Permanent Labour Tribunal Act as early as possible. This I knew involved the investigatory and the adjudicatory processes, which might last from a year to two years. Secondly, I planned to get my lawyers to process a court injunction to enable me to continue to occupy the company house. I was aware that without a fighting space I would not be able to continue with the struggle. Thirdly, I was going to seek an audience with the Board of Directors of FAL in order to determine their position on the matter and possibly to get reinstated. Finally, bearing in mind that I was not receiving any income in a period of great economic hardship nationally, and also knowing the theoretical stand of the Party and State leadership on women's rights, I planned to approach any other relevant persons and institutions whose intervention I deemed to be critical in order to secure an early reinstatement. I thought my case deserved this multi-pronged approach.

February 1985

The day I was dismissed I wrote to the JUWATA branch at FAL to inform them that I intended to take my case before the Permanent Labour Tribunal (PLT), in accordance with the Permanent Labour Tribunal Act No. 41 of 1967. In doing so I was seeking their support. This was necessary since by definition a trade dispute is only said to exist if it involves two or more employees. Section 4(1) of the PLT Act states:

> Any trade dispute, whether existing or apprehended if not otherwise determined may be reported to the Labour Commissioner by notice in writing given either by, or on behalf

of the employees by the General Secretary of a registered Trade Union of which the employees are members.

Since I was taking my case before the Labour Commissioner as a single employee, the support of the JUWATA branch ensured that the dispute enjoyed a collectivity of interest; it ceased to be the dispute of a single employee.

The Union replied that it was in support of my dispute for two good reasons. Firstly, the company management had not carried out the mandatory consultations as required by the law under Section 6(1)g of the Security of Employment Act before it declared me redundant. The Union had only been informed that I would no longer be working with FAL a few hours after I was dismissed. The Union and Management had then proceeded to discuss the impending redundancies of all other company employees. Secondly, they reasoned that if the company's statement that I had been removed solely on cost-reduction considerations was true, then the fact that the company had proceeded to appoint another employee, an expatriate, to head the newly reconstituted Finance and Administration Department, and who was going to earn eight times the salary I was earning, negated the whole purpose of the exercise.

After writing to the JUWATA branch at FAL, I set the wheels in motion to get a court injunction in a bid to keep a fighting space. The company had given me only seven days to vacate the house, and without the house it was going to be very difficult for me to engage in a protracted struggle.

The town where I live, Arusha, like many other towns in Africa, has an acute shortage of housing. Looking for alternative accommodation at such short notice was going to be very hard indeed. In consideration of this, I visited my lawyers for the second time and requested them to process a court injunction to enable me to continue to live in the company house, pending the outcome of the Tribunal proceedings. Mr Mwale, who had worked on the earlier injunction, wasted no time in drafting a plaint and filing an application for an ex-parte hearing (a hearing of the applicant only). This was deemed expedient since the matter required urgent intervention by the court. On 26 February 1985 the Resident Magistrate's Court in Arusha issued a temporary injunction prohibiting the General Manager of FAL from evicting me until the matter was heard and decided upon.

As a close follow-up to the two actions outlined above, I decided to adhere to the regulations of SCOPO which require an employee to appeal to the Board of Directors if he or she feels they have been unfairly dismissed. The letter effecting my dismissal had not indicated that the General Manager of FAL was acting on behalf of the FAL Board who was legally my employers. Rather the letter had made vague reference to TWICO's letter. My relationship with TWICO was not a direct one, and nor was TWICO my employer. And the fact that the letter ordering my dismissal had come from what I considered by now to be enemy territory left me in no doubt that the General Manager of TWICO had personally engineered my dismissal. Knowing that I probably did not stand much chance of reversing my position, I still felt obliged, as a matter of procedure, to write to the Chairman of the FAL Board, who was also the General Manager of TWICO, to inform him of my intention to appeal to the Board. As can be seen, TWICO's General Manager was in a good position to thwart my attempts to achieve reinstatement. He straddled both Boards and as Chairman of the FAL Board, had greater personal access to the members of that Board. As a chief executive of TWICO, too, he attended the meeting of the TWICO Board of Directors. Nevertheless I wrote to him informing him that I had been unfairly dismissed and that I was seeking his audience and that of the Board so that I could put my case before them. A copy of this letter was mailed to all the other Board members. In a separate letter, I requested the General Manager of FAL to include my appeal on the agenda for the next Board meeting.

It is indicative of the true state of affairs that I never received a letter of acknowledgment from the Chairman of the FAL Board, the Board members or the General Manager of FAL. Consequently I was never invited to meet the Board. I did not find that surprising. The Board met on 18 May 1985, but according to a reliable source was unable to come to agreement on the issue of my dismissal. I was very disappointed that the Board could just ignore my appeal after ten years' service. That put an end to my hopes that I might get redress through the Board of Directors.

Before I conclude with this month, it is worth pointing out that on 21 February 1985 I received a letter from the General Manager of FAL ordering me to come back and relinquish my duties!

March 1985

In the meantime, the JUWATA branch officials at FAL had got in touch with the officials of JUWATA at the district level, indicating that they were supporting my case against the company and stating their reasons for doing so. The District Secretary of

JUWATA then wrote to the General Manager of FAL informing him that until such time as my case was decided by the Permanent Labour Tribunal, I was still a bona fide company employee and as such was entitled to live in the company house. He further informed him of the JUWATA opinion that the procedure for declaring me redundant was improper. In reply, the General Manager of FAL showed that he was unaware of the stand adopted by the JUWATA branch because four days later he wrote to the District JUWATA Secretary informing him that JUWATA had been involved and had accepted my dismissal. Furthermore, on the matter of housing, the General Manager informed the District JUWATA Secretary that he should not interfere in the internal affairs of the company!

The next letter from the District JUWATA Secretary requested a meeting between the General Manager of FAL, the JUWATA Branch Chairman, the JUWATA Branch Secretary and himself to discuss my case. The date of the meeting was specified and I was also told to attend. The General Manager of FAL did not show up; instead he sent a letter disclaiming responsibility for dismissing me and directing the District JUWATA Secretary to contact the officials of the holding company, TWICO, who he said were my employers and bore sole responsibility for dismissing me. Towards the end of March the District Secretary wrote to FAL's General Manager once more, thanking him for his previous reply but also insisting that they meet to discuss my dismissal notwithstanding that the decision to remove me had been ordered by the holding company.

While all this was going on I went to court to fight for custody of my youngest daughter who was then two and a half years old. My unemployment had provided a good opportunity for my husband to humiliate and ridicule me even further by striving to deprive me of my last source of company, on the grounds that I did not have the financial means to shoulder responsibility for her care.

April 1985

In his reply to the District JUWATA Secretary the General Manager of FAL reiterated his earlier position emphasising that the decision to dismiss me had come from TWICO. It was TWICO, the letter said, which had ordered the rationalisation of the company's organisational structure. He stated that it was not within his powers to deal with the matter and he regretted that he would not be able to participate in further discussion or correspondence. With this note of finality the case could proceed to the next level: the regional Union level. The District JUWATA Secretary wrote to the Regional JUWATA Secretary informing him of my case and of his office's unsuccessful effort to get the matter resolved. In his opinion, the District Secretary wrote, TWICO had no legal power to order my dismissal because I was an employee of FAL which is a legally constituted company and a separate entity from TWICO. He further added that the requirement to consult with the Union had not been adhered to. He recommended that the regional office deal with the matter expeditiously.

The Regional Secretary did not call for a meeting with the General Manager of FAL; instead he wrote to him raising five points which required clarification. These were: firstly, to explain why it was necessary for the General Manager of FAL to write me a letter of dismissal if the General Manager of TWICO, whom he claimed was my employer, could have legally written such a letter himself; secondly, to state explicitly if this decision had been sanctioned by the Board of Directors of FAL which was my legal employing authority; thirdly, to explain whether the functions of the position of Personnel and Administrative Manager had also been abolished; fourthly, whether, in his own opinion, as General Manager of FAL he had legal power to dismiss me; and finally, whether the mandatory requirement to consult with JUWATA had been observed. One month later, there had been no reply from the General Manager of FAL.

May 1985

The matter could now proceed to the next level, the national JUWATA office. In his letter to the Secretary General, the Regional Secretary detailed my educational background and work experience, the relationship between FAL and TWICO and the reasons why he deemed my dismissal to be unfair. Finally he requested that a trade dispute be declared between JUWATA on my behalf and FAL.

Towards the middle of the month, the temporary injunction that had enabled me to continue occupying the company house was withdrawn because of a successful application filed by my employers through a private solicitor to get my case determined on merit. This request was not unusual and moreover it did not mean that I was therefore to be evicted. My plea for a temporary injunction had been heard ex-parte, and now the court would conduct a hearing of the main suit with both parties in attendance. I was still, therefore, the applicant.

On the date set for the hearing of the main suit my solicitor was taken ill, so I decided to go to court to request an adjournment. When I reached the courthouse, I saw the defendants' solicitor go into court, and being unsure of court protocol I decided to wait for the court clerk to call me in also. (I still had this unfounded but not uncommon fear of the courts.) I was astounded, therefore, when the defendants' solicitor came out of court and informed me that my application had been dismissed. This meant that I was now an easy target for eviction, since the basis for an injunction had been removed. It was so incredible that for some minutes my mind refused to function. Gathering my wits together I reasoned that if I wanted to continue to occupy this house I would have to act fast to have my case reinstated.

That same day, I succeeded in filing another application which was meant to restore Civil Cause No. 33 of 1985 to the Register so that the original application could be heard on its merit. In effect it was an application within an application. In my application I requested the indulgence of the court to set aside the order for dismissal of my application and fix a fresh hearing date.

Three days later, I stood against a very experienced lawyer (my solicitor was still indisposed) to argue my case as to why I was requesting a restoration of my application. I argued that I could not have foreseen that my solicitor would be ill, and because of this, had come to request an adjournment. I said that I had been surprised to be told that my case had been dismissed. I also pleaded that I was very inexperienced when it came to court matters and that I had actually been standing outside the court waiting for the court clerk to usher me in when the defendants' lawyer had entered the court chamber.

The defendants' solicitor attempted to intimidate me; he had me sworn in and he proceeded to subject me to a barrage of questions. I stuck to my original position with regard to what I stated above. Judgment was instant. After listening to both sides the magistrate accepted my explanation and my application was reinstated.

With that decided, I could stay on in the house until the hearing of the main suit. I breathed a little more easily after that but my position was not a happy one. Not only did I feel hounded on all sides, it was as if an unseen sword were waiting to descend on my neck.

June 1985

The Secretary General of JUWATA wrote to the Labour Commissioner in the Ministry of Labour and Manpower Development asking him to declare a trade dispute. He attached all the relevant documents relating to my case. A copy of this letter was sent to me. The relevant section of the Permanent Labour Tribunal Act was Section 9A (1) which provides that:

> Subject to subsection (2) where any trade dispute exists or is apprehended, the Labour Commissioner may inquire into the causes and circumstances of the trade dispute and with the approval of the Minister refer any matters appearing to him to be connected with or relevant to that trade dispute to the Tribunal and the Tribunal shall inquire into the matters referred to it and report on them to the Minister.

During this month, I won custody of my last-born, despite the fact that I was still not employed. I decided not to press for maintenance.

July 1985

The Labour Commissioner wrote to the General Manager of FAL enquiring into the matter of my dismissal. In his reply the General Manager stated that I had been an employee of TWICO from 1976 until 1985 when my services were terminated. The letter went on in the same deceitful vein stating that the Union branch had been involved in the exercise to declare me redundant, and that my services had been terminated by TWICO. It was interesting to see how the General Manager of FAL kept repeating 'my company', 'my Union branch' and that what he had done was in the 'national interest' since the economic problems of Tanzania were all too well known. He added that the action to 'abolish' my department was intended to reduce costs and increase efficiency and was not prompted by hatred, conspiracy or ill motives as I claimed.

Towards the middle of July, I went to the United Nations Women's Decade Conference in Nairobi as a member of the government delegation. Being away from Arusha I was able to look at my situation in a much broader perspective. The conference was on the themes of equality, development and peace, which were examined in the context of the achievements and obstacles still preventing the attainment of equality between women and men. And here I was, contending with forces external and internal to my work which seemed determined to make me less equal, retard my development and disturb my peace. I came out of the conference determined to pursue the case to the bitter end. I also came out of it convinced that no one was going to assist me in this crusade. It was up to me to use the existing laws to redress this wrong.

August 1985
I decided to look for a temporary job to augment my diminishing savings and by good fortune I found work with the Danish Volunteer Training Centre on the outskirts of Arusha.

October 1985
The Labour Commissioner wrote to the JUWATA Secretary General enclosing the reply from the General Manager of FAL and enquiring if the Secretary General was still in favour of declaring a trade dispute. The Secretary General wrote in the affirmative and requested that the matter be expedited.

In mid-October I left Arusha for Helsinki to represent the Centre for Integrated Rural Development in Africa (CIRDAFRICA) at a meeting on the formulation of checklists and guidelines for use in planning, administering and implementing development programmes and projects. My awareness of women's problems was strengthened, but with an added dimension: now the problems of women in agriculture in a cross-cultural perspective were shown to me for the first time.

November 1985
The Danish Volunteer Training Centre suddenly told me to resign or else face dismissal on the grounds that it no longer needed my services. On further investigation I learnt that my husband had paid the Principal a visit while I was away in Finland. I confronted the Principal with this fact but he refused to discuss what had transpired, saying only that he was afraid to have legal steps taken against the Centre. By the end of November I was once more without a job.

I went for an interview with the Tanzania Textile Corporation (TEXCO) in Dar es Salaam for the position of Manpower Development and Administrative Manager which had been advertised in the *Daily News*. During the interview I was asked about my past employment and why I wanted to be employed by TEXCO. My reply was that I had been working with Fibreboards (Africa) Limited for ten years, but that my services had been terminated due to cost-reduction measures. Now, I explained, I needed a job. I felt that I had the relevant qualifications and experience, which I wanted to put to good use, and that I had nothing in my background to be ashamed of. Moreover, I had taken my dispute before the Permanent Labour Tribunal to prove that I had been unfairly dismissed. While I was talking I did not feel as confident as I sounded. Had I been in the interviewers' position, I too would have been sceptical about someone whose services were dispensed with after ten years of employment. Moreover, at that point I had no idea if I was going to win the dispute. So I simply crossed my fingers and wished myself good luck.

December 1985

The Labour Commissioner wrote to the Minister for Labour and Manpower Development detailing facts pertaining to my case and pointing out that JUWATA at all levels was in support of the dispute. He recommended that an inquiry be conducted by the Permanent Labour Tribunal to look into the allegations that my dismissal was unfair, under Section 9A (1) of Permanent Labour Tribunal Act No. 41 of 1967 and that ultimately a ruling be given by the Minister under Section 9B (1) of the same Act.

Section 9B (1) of the Permanent Labour Tribunal Act states:

> Upon receipt of the report made by the Tribunal in respect of any matter referred to it under Section 9(A) the Minister shall make a decision in relation to the matters contained in the report, and that decision shall be final.

Towards the end of the month, I was recalled for another interview with TEXCO. Two days later I was informed by two top company directors that I had passed the interview and that I would be employed to work in one of their subsidiaries in Morogoro Town as the Manpower Development and Administrative Manager. They proceeded to brief me about the company and to explain what my job entailed. When I left the TEXCO premises that day I felt sure I had landed a good job. I invited my few friends in Dar es Salaam to come out for a celebration and when I reached Arusha I started to make arrangements for packing and disposing of some of my things ready for the move to Morogoro. I even notified my young daughter's teacher that we would be leaving the area so that she could arrange to fill her place by February.

January 1986

The Minister of Labour wrote to the Chairman of the Permanent Labour Tribunal bringing to his attention the preliminary inquiry made by the Labour Commissioner. In his letter the Minister specified the terms of reference under which the inquiry would be held:

1. Why the intention to dismiss me had not been communicated to JUWATA before I was declared redundant in the same manner as for other employees.
2. If I would have been able to be the head of a newly reconstituted department if a competent subordinate had been found to deal with financial matters.
3. If an expatriate had been employed who earned foreign exchange and other fringe benefits amounting to eight times more than my earnings.
4. Whether the position of Manpower Development and Administrative Manager had been abolished in all TWICO subsidiaries.
5. Whether the termination of my services was motivated by victimisation, hatred and conspiracy.
6. Whether it would not have been possible for me to be assigned other duties within TWICO itself or other TWICO subsidiaries.
7. Whether I was given a hearing with my company's Board of Directors.
8. Whether I should be reinstated.

The letter also named the assessors, all resident in the Arusha region, who would assist the Chairman of the Tribunal in his inquiry.

When the Minister's letter reached the Permanent Labour Tribunal offices, the Registrar wrote to both the Secretary General of JUWATA and to the General Manager of FAL requiring them each to submit a memorandum on the dispute within a fortnight and also to exchange copies of their memoranda. Failure to submit a memorandum, both were told, would not deter the Tribunal from conducting a hearing.

The memorandum from JUWATA specified the grounds on which it intended to demonstrate that the dismissal of my services had been unfair. These were:

1. That the action of TWICO to order my dismissal was *ultra vires* in so far as I was not an employee of TWICO but of Fibreboards (Africa) Limited. Only the Board of Directors of FAL had such powers after taking into consideration all the relevant factors pertaining to my employment.

2. That JUWATA was especially concerned about the discriminatory treatment meted out to me, particularly in comparison with that of heads of other departments which had also been similarly abolished.
3. That in their haste to get rid of me, management had forgotten that I was the manager in charge of personnel matters and thus a key figure in the exercise of redundancy. Even if it was management's intention to declare me redundant, this would have been the last step, after I had participated in the whole exercise of redundancy. The fact that I was removed prior to the whole exercise smacked of a conspiracy.
4. That JUWATA at the branch level was *not consulted* as required under Section 6(1)g of the Security of Employment Act. JUWATA at branch level was only informed of my removal. (*my emphasis*)
5. Finally JUWATA demanded that I be reinstated without loss of benefits from the day my services were terminated, because the dismissal was unfair, and that the newly employed expatriate be removed forthwith.

The employers' defence drafted by a senior counsel of Tanzania Legal Corporation (a state-owned body), came out ferociously against my reinstatement. In it FAL advanced the following eight points:

1. That Fibreboards (Africa) Limited was not responsible for terminating my services but that the holding corporation, TWICO, had directed some of its subsidiaries to abolish their Manpower Development and Administration Departments, of which FAL was one of the affected subsidiaries. For reasons of efficiency and economy it was necessary that the Manpower Development and Administration Departments be merged with Finance. The fact that only four subsidiaries were affected was a result of the contract existing between the governments of Tanzania and Finland whereby Finland provided management expertise to some of TWICO's subsidiary companies. *The reorganisation of company structure was a consequence of their advice*. (*my emphasis*)
2. Since my department had been abolished, I had to be retired. *TWICO had no other place for me*. The expatriate who was employed to head the Finance and Administration Department at FAL was being paid by EKONO [the Finnish

firm providing expert advice to FAL], which was currently managing FAL. My retirement had nothing to do with the Indian expatriate. (*my emphasis*)
3. TWICO's action to order my dismissal was not *ultra vires* because I was earning a salary that put me directly under TWICO's jurisdiction.
4. That the abolition of a department is not a disciplinary matter. It only means retiring all the workers in that department, although in this case not all were retired. Since *my* department was abolished, I could not have been relied upon to contribute impartially to the redundancy exercise. So JUWATA's claim that I should have participated was baseless.
5. That, to elaborate further, I was not the only person to be retired but many other workers were affected. If this redundancy exercise was unfair to me, then it was equally unfair to the other employees who were made redundant.
6. In totality all claims by JUWATA were vehemently denied because they were baseless.
7. That the cost-reduction exercise was ordered by the Government. All the redundancy procedures were adhered to.
8. That the Union branch at FAL had not made any representations on my behalf. This could only be interpreted to mean that the Union was in agreement with the cost-reduction measures taken by management, including my dismissal.

Both the Union and the employers had filed their claims and counterclaims with the Permanent Labour Tribunal and it was now possible to set a hearing date. That date was 14 March 1986. In the meantime I received a letter from TEXCO regretting that it could not employ me. Since the letter offered no explanation for this rejection I immediately left for Dar es Salaam to find out from company officials what was going on. I met one of the directors who had briefed me on TEXCO operations. He was apologetic, uncomfortable and evasive. On the same day, a Tuesday, I made an appointment through his personal secretary to see TEXCO's top official the following Saturday at 8.30 a.m. When I returned on Saturday for the appointment I was told that the official was too busy to see me! Once more my hopes of earning a proper income were shattered. I returned to Arusha heartbroken and almost despairing, but hopeful that the Labour Tribunal would bring some good tidings for a change.

5

Before I go into details of the Tribunal hearing itself, I want to touch briefly on the other forms of action that I took and the opportunities that presented themselves to me as I nursed expectations of an earlier solution to my problem.

I appealed first to the first President of the United Republic of Tanzania, Mwalimu ('Teacher') Julius Nyerere. More than anyone else in the State and Party leadership, Nyerere had written and talked quite extensively on the question of promoting equality between women and men. In fact it can be postulated that a significant proportion of the rights enjoyed by Tanzanian women today could be attributed to Nyerere personally. Apart from writing specifically about equality, even his general writings contain messages of significance for women. For example, the following is to be found in the 1971 Party Guidelines:

> Any action which gives people more power of decision and domination over their own lives is an act of development, even if it does not increase health or food. Any action which decreases the power of decision and domination over their own lives is against development, it retards the people even if it adds to their health and food.

Such fighting statements can be used by women as a defence against male colonialism.

Even more relevant was Nyerere's speech to the African regional preparatory meeting for the World Conference of the United Nations Decade for Women held in Arusha in October 1984. I attended the meeting as part of the government delegation. The following is extracted from the President's speech:

> But [the] women are also victims of exploitation by African societies – societies ruled by men . . . World-wide experience of political and civil rights for women has also demonstrated the limitations as well as the importance of legislation. It

> shows that, if these legal rights are to be meaningful in their lives, women have to acquire social and economic power as well as education and training. Social attitudes militate against women's development from the earliest stages of social life . . . social attitudes and the educational content in schools subtly direct girls towards the virtues of subservience and service to men. Girls are not treated as having equal rights, and because they are human beings must grow up accepting and conforming to the expectations of the society in which they live . . .
>
> Women's development . . . involves the application in reality of equal employment opportunities. In particular it means building new social attitudes in which all people are regarded as of equal social worth, so that the criteria for the allocation of private and public responsibilities is not sex but the individual's abilities and potential contribution.

It is clear from the above that the President possessed great awareness of the factors militating against equality between women and men. What made me take the decision to appeal to him personally, however, was the following, quoted from the same speech:

> The history of the world shows that the oppressed can get allies and need to get allies from the dominant group as they wage their struggle for equality, human dignity and progress . . . You have allies. I will continue to try to be one of them.

I and the other women present were moved by this speech and gave Nyerere a standing ovation lasting many minutes. Now it seemed that the battle I was waging against my employers had all the ingredients of a struggle for equality, human dignity and respect. And so, when I wrote to the President explaining at great length that I had been unfairly dismissed and appealing for his merciful intervention, I invoked his promise to be an ally of the oppressed. I even flew to Dar es Salaam with the intention of seeing him if it were possible. At the State House, the President's official residence, I was directed to see a certain official who asked why I wanted to see the President. I explained my problem, whereupon the official told me that he would try to see that my letter reached the President. That was early in March 1985.

Four months later, on 13 July 1985, I received a letter from that same official. He regretted the delay in giving me a reply and went on to say that, after consulting his boss, he was instructed to direct me to the Ministry of Labour and Manpower Development, which had been given full powers to deal with complaints arising out of the cost-reduction exercise. Copies of the letter had been sent to the Principal Secretary to the Ministry of Labour and to the Secretary General of JUWATA. There was no indication whether any details accompanied those letters. Nor did I hear from the two offices, except in their functions in relation to the dispute through the Labour Tribunal.

In effect the President had not been allowed to see my letter. Could it be that he and those around him did not think alike on equality? I surmised that the President sees only what those close to him deem appropriate for him to see. To them my letter did not merit the President's attention. The advice to take my case to the Ministry of Labour was superfluous as my case was already proceeding in that direction. The reason I wanted a quick intervention by the President was to save myself and my family from starvation. I still confidently believe that had the President been allowed to see my letter he would have acted in my favour.

The second personal appeal that I made was to the Tanzania Women's Union. In Tanzania there is a single women's organisation known as Umoja wa Wanawake wa Tanzania (UWT). It is affiliated to the only political party – Chama cha Mapinduzi. The main office bearer is the Secretary General who is appointed by the Chairman of the Party. She is assisted by two Deputy Secretary Generals, one from Tanzania Mainland and the other from the Isles.

I made an effort to link up with the Women's Organisation in order to create a network of support and solidarity in my struggle against discrimination and victimisation. I saw it as having the capacity to appeal effectively to higher authorities and to secure me an early reinstatement. However, in my opinion, the role of the Women's Organisation tends to be limited by the patriarchal bureaucratic structure within which it has to operate and by a low level of feminist consciousness among the women themselves, though the organisation has effectively campaigned for specific women's rights with quite a good record of success. The amendments made to the provisions of the Employment Ordinance in 1975 that favoured women, for example, can in part be credited to the Women's Organisation. And so too can the Musoma Resolution which waived the requirement that girls work for two years before entering university. The Women's Organisation's leaders have again and again exhorted the State and Party leadership to give greater responsibilities in decision-making positions to women of ability in order to give policy-making a more balanced approach.

Moreover the constitution of the Women's Organisation states the following among its main objectives:

> UWT is an instrument for safeguarding, developing and promoting respect for equality throughout the nation.
>
> UWT is an instrument for the emancipation of the women of Tanzania from exploitation and from traditions that retard their development and the development of the nation.

Bearing all these factors in mind, I wrote to the Secretary General of UWT acquainting her with my predicament. In doing this I had the support of the regional UWT officials, who were convinced that my case could only be dealt with successfully at the highest level.

My letter to the Secretary General contained a brief history of my educational and work experience and also detailed the reasons why I thought my case was based on victimisation and not on cost-reduction considerations. I pointed out that in a nation where Party and State leadership and UWT have been clamouring and canvassing for higher responsibilities for women, I was the only woman manager at FAL and the only manager to be dismissed under the cost-reduction exercise.

The Secretary General received my letter very sympathetically and invited me to Dar es Salaam to see her, paying my air fare and making arrangements for my case to be dealt with at the highest office in the land. In the hope that my case would be expeditiously solved, she sent me to the State House. There, however, I met the man whose junior had directed me to take my case to the Ministry of Labour and JUWATA. It was he who had prevented my letter from reaching the President. I came out of that meeting depressed; the discussion had led me up yet another blind alley.

On my way back from the State House, I tried to reflect on the proper strategy that UWT could have used in this case. Instead of consolidating its dependence on the male-dominated bureaucratic structures, UWT could have tried to use such an occasion to create its own platform. It would have been more effective, in my view, to have collected information on all the women who had been victimised under the cost-reduction exercise and to have carried out a public campaign against sex discrimination. I reasoned that publicising and politicising the issue would have had a long-term impact. On further reflection, however, I tried to appreciate the limitations imposed by the mode of the appointment to office of the Secretary General and her deputies. Having been appointed to office and not elected by their female constituency, how far could they go in pressing for the rights of their supposed constituency without affecting their own positions? And how far could they go in demanding equal rights for their members without acquiring the 'radical' label?

In July 1985 I had been to the United Nations Decade for Women Conference in Nairobi as a government delegate. What a contradiction that my contribution to the cause of women was recognised and acknowledged by women in high government positions yet I could not get proper acknowledgment of my own victimisation and my right to employment. Being part of the government delegation I was brought into contact with some of the most powerful women in Tanzania. I made sure that I talked with those women in the delegation, drawing their attention to my plight. Yet, one year after the Nairobi Conference, I was still struggling to get reinstated. Indeed, one of these so-called 'powerful' women told me quite plainly that she was afraid to antagonise men because ultimately it is men who appoint you to office. She advised me to go back to my parents and become a peasant!

Some women, however, did succeed in helping me. These women were equally powerful by virtue of their position in Government and the Party, though, as I came to learn later, they had had to act covertly. As they perceived it, my case contained more than met the eye on a preliminary appraisal. My enemies had access to a powerful network involving senior men in positions of authority. For the women who wanted to help me it was safer, therefore, that they try to speed up matters behind the scenes rather than give me open support which would have led to the more powerful forces swamping and submerging us all.

6

The hearing date was set by the Permanent Labour Tribunal for 14 March 1986, 13 months after my dismissal. Two weeks before this I received a letter of notification and immediately began to prepare a list of possible questions to be used to cross-examine the General Manager or his representatives. I was hampered at that time by the fact that I did not know who was going to represent the company at the hearing.

Three days before the hearing, the official from JUWATA headquarters who was to represent me arrived. I sought him out at his hotel and enquired about the strategy he intended to use to ensure success. He produced a copy of the memorandum he had filed with the Labour Tribunal and told me that he was going to argue the case on the basis of that memorandum. I asked him if it had occurred to him that he would be asked to cross-examine me and the witnesses for the applicant. He replied that this was unnecessary; the case was a straightforward one: I had been victimised and the submission he would make would bring this out clearly. According to him there would be no need for further courses of action. I enquired if he had ever had to represent someone before in a case of this nature. He told me that he had, and that the procedure was that he would read his submission and that would be the end of the matter.

I felt my heart sink. The Union headquarters had sent someone who was inexperienced and who did not know how to conduct himself before the Tribunal. Inwardly I began to panic. Perhaps this man had been chosen because of his sympathetic attitude towards my dispute. But what was needed to win the case was not sympathy but hard facts, properly and legally presented and argued. Calmly, I tried to explain to him what I understood the procedure to be. By that time I had familiarised myself thoroughly with the provisions of the Permanent Labour Tribunal Act. I was also a veteran of two tenancy cases and one child custody case at the Resident Magistrate's Court and had withstood cross-examination with some success. So I believed I knew what I was talking about. To convince the JUWATA official further, I took him to see a lawyer friend of mine. I asked my friend to help us to reframe the set of questions I had already prepared and to instruct the Union official on how to conduct himself before the Tribunal.

Luckily, the JUWATA official was an easy-going man. He listened and agreed to abide by our instructions. Together we rephrased the five sets of cross-examination questions: one for myself, one for the General Manager of FAL, one for the Administrative Officer I thought would be most likely to represent the company, and one for the Finnish Project Manager who normally deputised for the General Manager in his absence. Finally, I had prepared a set for the Union Branch Chairman of the company, who was going to be my witness.

That night the JUWATA official in his role as my solicitor/prosecutor, my friend acting as the Judge, my housemaid and daughter as observers and myself as the chief witness rehearsed our conduct in court. I was cross-examined, told to produce exhibits, told what and how much to say, told what to emphasise. The Union official was also shown how to behave, told not to repeat himself unnecessarily and to know when to ask something as a means of emphasis. Although we were light-hearted and laughed a lot, we knew in our hearts that the case was a serious one. Everyone present understood the importance I attached to my case. We got to bed in the early hours, including my three-and-half-year-old daughter.

Next day we contacted the JUWATA Branch Chairman, who was to be another JUWATA witness, so that he would know exactly what was required of him. We showed him the set of questions we had designed for him and together planned our strategies for winning the case. That night was the dress rehearsal in which we tried to improve the performance of the JUWATA official in his role as cross-examiner.

The hearing took place at the Arusha Regional Labour Office, where we assembled at nine o'clock on the morning of 14 March 1986.

The defendants were represented by a solicitor from Tanzania Legal Corporation, by the General Manager of FAL, and by the Company Secretary from TWICO. The fact that the company was represented by two people who held degrees in law did not disturb me at all. I believed that the case was heavily weighted in my favour. The Tribunal was composed of the Chairman of the Permanent Labour Tribunal, assisted by two Assessors representing the employer and JUWATA whose duty it was to advise the Chairman.

Members of the public were present too, including journalists from the nation's newspapers.

It would be impossible to describe the entire proceedings but I will try to bring out the main issues as they developed.

My side presented the case first, our objective being to show why we were claiming that my dismissal was unfair. In doing this we were to be guided by the terms of reference enumerated in the letter from the Minister of Labour (see page 60).

The JUWATA official cross-examined me initially in a manner that highlighted my qualifications, work experience and length of service with FAL. He then questioned me on how my dismissal had been effected, whether the Union and Management had met for consultations on redundancy. I replied that, as far as I was concerned, Management and the Union had met on 24 January 1985 to discuss measures to reduce costs and had agreed that workers would not be affected by these measures. I explained that the minutes given to me by the Union in reply to my letter of complaint showed that Management had met to discuss redundancy again only a few hours *after* I had been made redundant.

The Union official then questioned me on whether the relevant body, in this case the Board of Directors, had been consulted. My answer was that my letter of dismissal did not indicate that the Board had been consulted, or that the General Manager of FAL was acting on their behalf. It merely made reference to another letter from TWICO, which I had not been allowed to see though I had asked to do so.

The official then began to question me on the past experiences that had led me to perceive that I had been victimised. In reply I produced 20 pieces of evidence which I tendered as exhibits with lengthy explanations to prove that my dismissal had been for reasons other than cost-reduction considerations. These included:

> A memo to the General Manager of FAL requesting him to redefine my duties after his act of changing the list of personnel to be laid off during renovation, to which I had received no reply.
>
> Two internal memos written to me by my subordinate, the Administrative Officer, written at the direction of the General Manager, informing me of the General Manager's decision to remove all the company cars from the central administration pool.

A memo requesting clarification from the General Manager on the reallocation of company cars.

A memo to the General Manager explaining to him the difficulties experienced by my department due to this reallocation.

The letter from TWICO's General Manager ordering FAL to evict me from the company house within seven days, unless I produced a letter of permission from my husband or a divorce decree.

The minutes of the JUWATA committee expressing its concern over the issue of my eviction from the company house ostensibly at the request of my estranged husband.

A memo from the General Manager of FAL castigating JUWATA for trying to protect my housing rights.

A court injunction, restraining my employers from evicting me.

My letter to the General Manager of FAL informing him that I was not bound to obey the unlawful orders of the General Manager of TWICO.

The telex from TWICO's General Manager requesting information on my movements.

A reply to that telex from FAL's General Manager.

My memo to the General Manager of FAL requesting him to seek the source of the insults heaped upon me by the Finnish Project Manager, to which there was no reply.

My second memo on the same subject to which there was no reply.

My letter to TWICO's General Manager requesting clarification of the information given to me by the Finnish Project Manager that TWICO/FAL intended to employ an administrative specialist and abolish my department.

My evidence at this point was intended to demonstrate that the moves to dismiss me had been contemplated long before my dismissal was effected. The actions of the General Manager in humiliating me by refusing to acknowledge my queries and by bypassing me in favour of my subordinates, I pointed out, were calculated to demoralise, demean and degrade me and lead to my resignation. I said that in law this is called constructive dismissal. I explained also that the General Manager of TWICO, on the other hand, had sent a telex in a bid to establish grounds for summarily dismissing me.

The JUWATA representative then led me through a cross-examination which revealed how I understood that my dismissal had been ordered by the General Manager of TWICO and not by the Board of Directors of FAL. I stated that the Board, on the other hand, had not reacted to the letter that I had written to them immediately after my dismissal, praying for their intervention. I pointed out that the General Manager of TWICO was also the Chairman of the FAL Board of Directors. I argued that though his letter to me had stated that my position had been abolished, it did not mean that my duties or the personnel functions had disappeared or even diminished. I said that I believed that so long as FAL had not ceased to exist my duties were still in existence. I pointed out that I had received a letter from the General Manager of FAL ordering me to hand over my duties to the Administrative Officer. I went on to inform the Tribunal that the principle of First In, Last Out had not been adhered to because in comparison with the other officer who was left to perform the personnel functions, I was senior not only in terms of length of service but also in terms of qualifications. I further went on to say that of the three managers whose departments had been similarly abolished I was the only one who had been declared redundant. The two other managers had been reallocated junior positions and continued to work at FAL. This option had not been extended to me. I pointed out that this was discrimination against me as a woman.

I was asked to inform the Tribunal if, during my working life, I had ever been reprimanded by the Board. I replied that I had never been given any reprimand by the Board. On being asked if I knew whether FAL had employed an expatriate after my dismissal I said that the minutes from JUWATA showed that an Indian expatriate had been employed after my dismissal to head the new Finance and Administration Department. The JUWATA minutes were tendered as an exhibit. The JUWATA official's question on whether there were many women managers at FAL was overruled on grounds that the Tribunal was not a political forum.

After that, the company's counsel was given an opportunity to cross-examine me. His technique was to attempt to prove that the company had been right to dismiss me because I did not have the qualifications the company needed! He asked me if I held a professional qualification in accounts. I said I did not. Then he decided to go for the jugular by asking me a series of questions that would cast doubt on my testimony. He asked me if I was married. I replied in the affirmative. He asked me if I was still living with my husband. I replied in the negative. He wanted to know why I was not staying with my husband. I said my reasons were personal. At this juncture the Tribunal Chairman asked him not to continue with this line of questioning as the Tribunal was not a marriage conciliation board. The company's counsel's questions did not unravel anything new because, like an old and defective record, I kept repeating what I had said before. By the end of his cross-examination I felt that instead of destroying me, my opponent's counsel had given me more room to make explicit points not brought out during the initial cross-examination. My presentation lasted for three and a half hours. The members of the public, including the journalists, were still there.

In the afternoon session it was the turn of the other JUWATA witness, the Branch Chairman of the Union at FAL. Our strategy had been to lead him to produce the kind of evidence that would show that Management had not adhered to the requirement to consult with the Union and also that the Union was supporting my claim that I had been unfairly dismissed. The Branch Chairman pointed out that before the reorganisation, the Personnel Department was superior to the Finance Department because the Finance Department would never effect any payment unless it was sanctioned by either the General Manager or the Personnel Manager. He went on to inform the Tribunal that he was surprised that after my dismissal, the company had recruited an expatriate who was paid much more than I was. His evidence confirmed that JUWATA did not support Management's action in recruiting an expatriate in a situation where the main objective was to cut costs. Moreover, since the company had recruited the Indian expatriate, the industrial relations situation in the company had deteriorated because the expatriate was an accountant by profession and not conversant with the management of workers in any context, let alone the Tanzanian context; so much so that the General Manager was now *de facto* the Personnel Manager. By implication, concluded the JUWATA witness, what light did this evidence cast on the performance and competence of the incumbent Personnel office holders? At the end of this cross-examination, the hearing was adjourned until the next day.

The next day, 15 March 1986, it was the defendants' turn to present their case, the main representative being the General Manager of FAL. We had prepared 48 main questions for him, with expectations of formulating subsidiary questions for him as we went along. Members of the public and journalists were present. Our strategy here was to capitalise on what we considered to be his inadequacies and his infringement of the redundancy procedure.

After the cross-examination by learned counsel from Tanzania Legal Corporation, the JUWATA representative questioned the General Manager on his educational background. He said he had completed Standard Twelve. The JUWATA official wanted to know his work background and experience after school. He said that on leaving school he had joined the army, stayed there for ten years, and attained the position of captain. The advocate asked what his reason was for leaving the army. The reply was that the government had transferred him to the Ministry of Natural Resources in 1974. He was then asked why the government had found it fit to transfer him from the army to a civilian organisation. He said he did not know.

He was questioned as to whether he was confident in his position as General Manager of a company. He affirmed that he was. The cross-examination then proceeded as follows:

Q. If you are confident as a General Manager then how come you are implementing unlawful orders?
A. Which orders?
Q. You wrote a letter directing the applicant to vacate the company house within seven days?
A. I was obeying the orders of my boss, the General Manager of TWICO.
Q. You also abolished the position of Manpower Development and Administrative Manager at FAL without the Board's consent.
A. I did not. The order came from TWICO which is a holding company and which has jurisdiction over officers holding her position.
Q. Is your company a registered company under the law?
A. Yes.
Q. Does it possess the Memorandum and Articles of Association?

A. Yes.
Q. Do you have a Board of Directors separate from TWICO's Board of Directors?
A. Yes.
Q. Is your company a subsidiary or a branch of TWICO?
A. It is a subsidiary.
Q. As a subsidiary do you realise that the company is a separate legal entity, which can sue and be sued in its own right?
A. Yes. (*There was a pause to let the matter sink in.*)
Q. Tell us what you understand to be the requirements of the redundancy procedure.
A. Management should consult with JUWATA over redundancies.
Q. Is that all?
A. Yes.
Q. What about the principle of First In, Last Out?
A. That as well.
Q. You have two people who were senior in the Personnel Department, one is the applicant and the other is the Administrative Officer. Who was most senior? Who was employed first?
A. The applicant was most senior. She was employed first. (*A pause.*)
Q. You said you have a Board of Directors?
A. Yes.
Q. How did they feature in the removal of the applicant?
A. They blessed it.
Q. Congratulations! Could you give us the relevant Board minutes?
A. I do not have it. Oh, I think it is in my briefcase. (*The Chairman of the Tribunal ordered that the General Manager have access to his briefcase. For five minutes he rummaged through his briefcase. No doubt he was struggling with his conscience on whether he should produce the minutes or not. I was very close to him and could see that he had the minutes right there. Finally he decided to produce the minutes. The minutes were handed to the JUWATA official for scrutiny. We knew what we were looking for.*)
Q. The minutes accepting your proposal and confirming the applicant's dismissal show that the meeting of the Board was convened on 10 June 1985 while the applicant was dismissed on 20 February 1985. Is this how your Board operates?
A. I do not know. (*A pause and a change of tack.*)

Q. Is it true that there were seven departments before rationalisation?
A. Yes.
Q. And that these have been rationalised to four?
A. Yes.
Q. What happened to the other two managers whose departments were abolished?
A. They were reallocated other duties. (*A pause.*)
Q. Within FAL?
A. Yes. (*A longer pause and change of tack.*)
Q. Do you think abolition of a position is synonymous with abolition of duties?
A. Yes.
Q. If that is so then what it the Administrative Officer doing at FAL?
A. He is doing Personnel and Administrative work.
Q. Did you terminate, dismiss or retire the applicant?
A. She was retired.
Q. Is it normal for your company to remove within seven days employees who have been prematurely retired from company houses?
A. Yes.
Q. How long did Mr Ndamallya and Mr Kindiano, both company chief accountants, stay in the house after they had resigned?
A. Three months.
Q. How come the same courtesies were not extended to the applicant?
A. She did not request it. (*Grunts from the observers.*)
Q. Is it normal for your company to hold farewell parties for leaving senior officers?
A. Yes.
Q. Were parties held for the two chief accountants?
A. Yes.
Q. Were they held for the applicant who was being prematurely retired?
A. No.
Q. How come?
A. She did not request it. (*Laughter. Everyone in the court burst into laughter.*)
Q. Did the two accountants request it?
A. No.
Q. Were you in the habit of bypassing the applicant and asking her subordinate to direct her?

A. It was a matter of convenience.
Q. Do you agree that your convenience was demoralising the applicant?
A. I never thought about it.
Q. Did you receive this telex from the General Manager of TWICO concerning the applicant's whereabouts? (*showing him the telex*)
A. Yes.
Q. Do you consider it to be normal for the General Manager of a holding company to be so particular about an employee who is under the command of another General Manager?
A. It was the General Manager of TWICO's habit to do so because he considers the managerial personnel to be directly under his command.
Q. Can you produce a similar telex in relation to another manager in your company?
A. No.
Q. No more questions.

The last person to be interviewed was the Company Secretary. This testimony did not bring out anything new except the fact that he wanted to prove the impartiality of TWICO by showing that TWICO had ordered rationalisation of company structures throughout all its subsidiaries, which was not true. The Company Secretary pointed out that other personnel managers in other companies had been similarly affected. That was meant to make me feel good: we were equal in being disadvantaged, so I had nothing to complain about. My argument was different – TWICO had no business imposing its wishes on its subsidiaries without the consent of those subsidiaries' Boards. The FAL Board, on the other hand, had no business confirming my dismissal retrospectively. I had no wish to be a victim of their rubber-stamping actions. The hearing had ended.

7

Five months passed between the hearing and the delivery of the judgment. Why it took so long is anybody's guess, but it shows the weakness inherent in the labour legislation. The question I kept asking myself was how did these government bureaucrats expect me to survive in these hard economic times without any income? Was this their way of throwing me into total despair?

Towards the end of March, *Mfanyakazi*, a weekly newspaper owned and published by the JUWATA, wrote about my case under the heading 'The JUWATA demands that the Manager be reinstated'. In this article the JUWATA paper expressed great indignation at the employment of the Indian expatriate immediately after my dismissal under the cost-reduction exercise. It also reiterated JUWATA's submission that my dismissal had been occasioned by hatred, victimisation and conspiracy between the General Managers of TWICO and FAL. The paper further asserted that it was inconceivable that a public servant of my calibre who had been educated at great expense by the state should be dismissed without a valid reason.

It might have been expected that such a report would have galvanised the government watchdogs into action to follow up the case and see that it received immediate attention. Typically, however, it was like shouting in a storm.

When by June I had not received any information, I made a trip to Dar es Salaam to find out what was happening and my enquiries revealed that my file was neither at the Permanent Labour Tribunal offices nor at the Ministry of Labour. So although the Tribunal had agreed on its findings, somewhere along the corridors of power some individual or individuals had succeeded in preventing my file from finding its way to the Minister's table so that he could make a decision. I believe that this was done deliberately to frustrate and torture me as part of the grand conspiracy between my employers and their allies.

I did not see why the procedure for handling disputes could not have been specific about who could or could not handle the files on the way to the Minister. The Act should have provided a time limit for the proceedings in order to alleviate the possible difficulties that might be faced by an aggrieved employee.

Towards the end of June I began to feel depressed, doubtful and impatient. I felt that maybe I had wasted my time after all. I wondered how far the forces against me would go to manipulate the outcome. I was aware of their proximity to the relevant offices. I was also aware of their powerful formal and informal network. And whereas in the past I had been strongly convinced that I would win, I was now no longer confident. My spirits were temporarily revived by the appearance of my interview in the *Sunday News* with the apt title 'Why pick on me?' in which I explained my dissatisfaction with the manner in which I had been dismissed. I expected, after this public exposure, that the Women's Organisation would seize this moment to wage a public campaign against discrimination. However, it was another case of lost opportunity.

In July there was a mention of my interview on the Swahili Service of the BBC World Service in London, citing it as a classic example of wastage of skilled manpower in Third World countries.

But still there was no indication that the judgment was anywhere imminent. It was not until 7 August that I received a letter from the Arusha Regional Labour Officer informing me that the Minister's decision would be delivered by the Tribunal Chairman at the Regional Labour Office on 9 August 1986. On 8 August, at 8 a.m. as I was preparing to leave my house, I received a message to report immediately at the Labour Office. Judgment would be delivered that very morning because the Tribunal Chairman had other pressing commitments the following day.

We assembled in the Regional Labour Office at ten o'clock. The company was represented by the Administrative Officer. After a short while the Tribunal Chairman entered and began to read the Minister's Award. It was written in Kiswahili; the following is the literal translation:

Labour Dispute Inquiry No. 3 of 1986 between
JUWATA (on behalf of L. T. K. Mukurasi)
vs.
Fibreboards (Africa) Limited, Arusha

The Ruling

The report made after this inquiry shows that the applicant gained a Bachelor of Arts Degree at the University of Dar es

Salaam in 1975. Thereafter she worked for one year before joining Fibreboards (Africa) Limited as Administrative Officer. That is from 6 August 1976. In 1978 she was promoted to the position of Personnel and Training Officer. The employer sent her abroad for further training in Human Resources Management. She completed the course successfully and attained a Postgraduate Diploma in Personnel Management. Thereafter she was promoted to become the Manpower Development and Administrative Manager. This is the position she held until she was dismissed. She has also attended several seminars in Tanzania and abroad.

The applicant's services were terminated in February 1985. This step was taken as a measure to reduce costs. Whereas it was important that this be done, the applicant claimed before the Tribunal that the directive was used to legitimise acts of victimisation against her. During our inquiry into this dispute, we were able to uncover several actions that were meant to demoralise and degrade the applicant as a method of inflicting total despair. The evidence tendered showed that the General Manager had the habit of degrading the applicant in front of his junior officers and that he actually did bypass her, giving preference to her junior officer.

The other action that was meant to degrade the applicant was to order her to leave the company house on the grounds of her marital problems. It was improper to give her such an order on grounds that her husband had threatened to take the company to court. It would have held some elements of truth if the company had been prosecuted when it decided to let her continue to live in the company house.

The evidence produced during the inquiry into this dispute shows that after all these incidents the applicant wrote to the General Manager, seeking clarification of her obligations and rights as the Manpower Development and Administrative Manager. It was an act of utter scorn when the General Manager refused to reply.

The report shows that the defendants failed to adhere to Section 6(1) g of the Security of Employment Act No. 62 of 1964. As I have decided in other cases, failure to abide by this requirement in a redundancy exercise invalidates the entire exercise of redundancy. Moreover, the principle of First In, Last Out does not appear to have been adhered to in this case. The net result was to dismiss the applicant who was employed much earlier, leaving a more junior Administrative

Officer. Again non-observance of this principle invalidates the whole exercise of redundancy.

The report shows that the expatriate who was employed is paid by the Finnish government. His contract ends on 31 December 1986. Since the applicant was made redundant, and the principles of re-engagement dictate that redundant employees should have preference over all positions that become vacant, when the position of the expatriate becomes vacant it should be filled by the officer made redundant, who has the qualifications to fill such a position. The evidence tendered by JUWATA shows that since this expatriate took over as Finance and Administrative Manager the department has been beset by many problems to the extent that in effect the General Manager became the head of the Personnel Department. Since the applicant has had some experience in handling the accounts aspect, she may head the department.

In accordance with the findings of the inquiry and in relation to the issues raised that I deemed important and which formed the terms of reference, I want to emphasise the following in my award:

1. The employer did not carry out consultation with the JUWATA before dismissing the applicant, on the grounds that the applicant was not an employee of Fibreboards (Africa) Ltd. In reaching this conclusion the employer erred by not addressing himself as a General Manager of a legally independent company in relation to the applicant's employment. TWICO has authority over employees who were directly recruited by TWICO. If TWICO wished to have power over the applicant, TWICO should have transferred her to TWICO. Since this was not done, and since she was not with Fibreboards on secondment from TWICO, the employer who was obliged to adhere to the requirements of Sec. 6(1) g was Fibreboards (Africa) Ltd.
2. The Applicant should have been able to head the Finance and Administration Department. That position was given to an expatriate who was brought in under the contract that exists between the governments of Tanzania and Finland. I am directing that she be given the position of Administrative Officer or Personnel Officer until 31 December 1986 because she deserves first priority in filling the vacancies that come up after the redundancy exercise.
3. The expatriate was legally employed and is being paid in

foreign exchange by the Finnish government through the company known as EKONO OY.

4. It was not important to investigate this aspect.
5. From the evidence brought forward during the inquiry, the actions of the General Manager to demoralise and degrade her were proved. It became clear that these acts were the main basis for depriving her of the same treatment accorded to other managers whose positions were scrapped. The main reason for terminating her employment was occasioned by animosity against her. Management merely used the government directive as an excuse.
6. Since her employer was Fibreboards (Africa) Ltd., TWICO has no obligation to re-allocate her any duties. Neither have the other TWICO subsidiaries.
7. Since she was made redundant, even though the directive was made the excuse, she did not have to defend herself. To make one redundant means breaking her employment since the functions she was performing no longer exist and she cannot be allocated other functions. Since redundancy is not normally used as a punitive measure, the question of defending herself does not arise.
8. The applicant be re-assigned duties commensurate with other officers whose departments were affected by restructuring, as an assistant to the departmental head.
9. The applicant be reinstated as Personnel Officer from the day she was dismissed. When the expatriate's contract ends, she take over that position.

This award is given by me and is witnessed by my own hand here at Dar es Salaam today the 24th July 1986.

D. N. Mwakawago, MP
Minister of Labour and Manpower Development

You can imagine how I felt. I couldn't help thinking that the law had been judiciously and impartially applied. That evening we went for a celebration.

The events that had taken place between my dismissal and the successful outcome of the PLT hearing were no doubt interesting. The events that followed the hearing were even more interesting and, indeed, revealing. The fact that the Minister had ordered that I be reinstated was not the end of the matter, and the issue of my reinstatement would remain unresolved for a long time. Section 9B (1) of the Permanent Labour Tribunal Act stipulates that the decision of the Minister shall be final. In my case, as in several others, his decision did not prove to be final as we shall see in Part Three. I would now like to comment on the events recounted in Part Two.

It had taken 18 long months following my dismissal for me to be reinstated at the order of the Tribunal. For a victim who had no reliable source of income this had seemed like a lifetime. This is when I began to reflect quite seriously on the shortcomings of labour legislation which purports to protect workers' rights and interests. In the end the law defeats the sole purpose which it was meant to serve.

In the first instance, the investigatory stage proves to be long-drawn-out and arduous as the case progresses through the various JUWATA offices. There needs to be a definite time limit within which the case must reach the Minister of Labour and a final decision be made. Secondly, the requirement that a single aggrieved employee has support from JUWATA as a condition of a dispute being considered a trade dispute can prove tricky for certain categories of employees who may find themselves at the mercy of JUWATA. For example, the position of a personnel manager who has not appreciated the politics of her or his position as both a member of Management and a personification of Management to the workers could prove to be very difficult once she/he is in a position where Management has betrayed her/him and JUWATA decides to give her/him the cold shoulder. I need not elaborate here on the fact that the management of FAL and the Board of Directors had thrown me to the dogs. In my case it was JUWATA which saved me. Not every manager, whether of Personnel or another department, would find herself or himself in such a fortunate position.

My case also serves to demonstrate the imbalances in power existing among members of the state bureaucracy. Both the TWICO General Manager and the FAL General Manager were closer to the employer, the State, than I was and could thus pretend to act in the national interest. In addition, when I had taken action to procure an injunction to enable me to retain the company house until my case was decided by the Permanent Labour Tribunal, my employers had hired a private lawyer to oppose the granting of the injunction. And whereas I was paying counsel from my own funds, the General Manager of FAL could, and did, use company funds to pay a private lawyer. This contravened the SCOPO directive which prohibits the hiring of private advocates in preference to the services provided by Tanzania Legal Corporation. He could afford to do so, no doubt, because the Chairman of the Board, who is also the General Manager of TWICO, was behind him. At every point in the struggle these individuals were acting from a position of advantage, economically, whereas I was acting from a position of weakness.

I found it interesting that the Board of Directors of FAL did not bother to reply to my letter of complaint against my dismissal. This is less surprising, however, given that the General Manager of TWICO, who had engineered my dismissal, was also Chairman of the FAL Board of Directors. I had met the board members during my time at FAL, and they had struck me as fairminded men. I found it hard to comprehend that they could be swayed to act as a rubber stamp and accept my illegal dismissal four months after the event.

I encountered several women in top political positions during my fight and have come to the conclusion that being a woman and in a senior political position is not necessarily accompanied by a feminist consciousness. What had happened to me could happen to any woman. My case is not unique. Patriarchy and capitalism bolster one another up. My case apart, many women lost their jobs during the cost-reduction programme and the Women's Organisation could have used such incidents to its advantage by organising campaigns aimed at focusing public attention on the realities of discrimination against women in their working lives. Potentially these incidents could have had a transformatory effect. Such infringements of the rights of individual women contained elements capable of being combined into an issue of women's collective long-term political interests.

The women who might have politicised this issue appeared not to see the positive elements which might have enabled them to utilise it to benefit other women. While they recognised the potential the situation contained, they were also aware of their own positions within the patriarchal bureaucratic system which was responsible for putting them into the senior posts they held. Since the directive to reduce costs came from the top, it is possible that any action that could be sensed, even remotely, to be in opposition to this directive would be interpreted as subversive to the national interest. If this was the case, it is regrettable that those women in senior roles failed to make the distinction between the legitimate or neutral objectives of the directive and the subjective manner of its use or misuse in practice.

It is possible, however, that there is yet another explanation. As I continued to fight for my rights, as described in Part Three, I realised that I was fighting not against the personal discriminatory practices of the General Managers of TWICO and FAL but against other more powerful men in positions of authority behind them. The women whom I encountered in senior positions, being closer to these powerful men, were even more aware of their strength and perceived quite correctly that they were not evenly matched. If this was the case can they really be blamed for what they did, or rather failed to do?

PART THREE

Reinstatement and thereafter: the struggle continues

8

The Ministerial ruling which had been read in public by the Chairman of the Permanent Labour Tribunal on 8 August 1986 was given legal force by being duly registered by the Permanent Labour Tribunal, thus becoming an Award of the Permanent Labour Tribunal. The Certificate of Award for Trade Dispute No. 3 of 1986 between JUWATA (on behalf of L. T. K. Mukurasi) versus Fibreboards (Africa) Limited stated that:

(i) the allegations made in the application had been proved.
(ii) the employer's decision had been overruled.
(iii) the applicant was to be reinstated subject to the following conditions:
- to perform the duties of the Personnel Officer until such a time as the post of Finance and Administrative Manager should become vacant.
- to fill the position of Finance and Administrative Manager once it became vacant.
- to be reinstated on the same terms and conditions as obtaining prior to her dismissal.

Implicit in this ruling, though not clearly stated, was that reinstatement meant payment of my two years' salary in arrears. The Tanzanian *Daily News* carried a brief report of the Permanent Labour Tribunal ruling on its front page under the heading 'PLT orders Mukurasi's reinstatement'.

11 August 1986
I reported for duty and found the Acting General Manager in the office. This was the Finnish Project Manager who had vowed to sack me, and whose firm had been instrumental in offering advice to TWICO to rationalise the company's organisational structure. I had a letter prepared which informed the General Manager that I was reporting for duty in accordance with the terms of the PLT Award. I handed him my letter but he did not have much to say

to me. I left his office and spent part of the morning walking through the company compound, whose premises I had been forbidden to enter without permission. Everywhere I went the workers quietly greeted me as a heroine. They clenched their fists as a sign of victory and solidarity. In place of the spontaneous carefree atmosphere I had known, however, there was a lacklustre, subdued air about the place, no doubt engendered by fear of job loss which remained imminent because of the national economic crisis.

Two hours later I received a letter from the Acting General Manager instructing me not to come to the company premises because 'Management wanted to have time to consider the Labour Tribunal's Award'. The letter required me to come to FAL after 14 days to hear Management's decision. I was aware that FAL Management had no power to disobey this order but I was determined not to make waves. I wanted my reinstatement to be as smooth as possible. The tone of the letter, however, made me detect that there was going to be some resistance. If that was so I had to be ready to meet the challenge. I still had the inspiration, but I began to perceive that the mission might not be complete. Maybe what I had won was the battle but not the war. It remained to be seen.

On leaving the company's premises, I headed straight to my solicitor's office. James Mwale had by now become one of my pillars of strength. His reaction was immediate and swift. The next morning I went back to the factory with his letter to the Acting General Manager which said among other things:

> The judgment which was read in your presence was very clear that our client was to report immediately. It did not say that the company had fourteen days from the date of the award to make a decision, what decision? Any decision to the contrary would surely vary the decision of the Tribunal . . . The matter has reached the end and indeed it is high time that the company and our client shall start anew for the benefit of the company and the country.

There was no reaction from the Acting General Manager and from that time onwards I continued to report for duty. I was given neither an office nor duties, nor was I paid my salary arrears. I spent the first ten days or so hanging around the company compound.

18 August 1986
I was interviewed by Radio Tanzania, Swahili Service, about how I felt after my reinstatement and whether I was now settled and getting on well with my colleagues. My interview went out during the most interesting peak-hour session known as *Majira*, which is normally on the air at nine every night and discusses the day's events. I explained that I was happy to be back at FAL but that I had not been allocated an office nor been assigned any duties. Finally I pointed out that my salary arrears had not been paid in accordance with the orders of the Tribunal's Award.

20 August 1986
The substantive General Manager had come back to Arusha and I met him first thing in the morning. He allocated me an office, my old office within the Administration Building. For the next fortnight, I was neither allocated any duties nor paid my salary arrears as ordered by the Tribunal. Nevertheless I continued to report for duty.

25 August 1986
I reported to the Regional JUWATA Secretary that I had not received my salary arrears. The Regional Secretary said he would find a way of dealing with the matter.

28 August 1986
The Regional Secretary informed me he had contacted the Regional Labour Officer who in turn had contacted the Chairman of the Labour Tribunal. The Chairman of the Tribunal, who happened to be in Arusha, then wrote to the Principal Resident Magistrate asking the Resident Magistrate's Court in Arusha, a court of competent jurisdiction, to endorse an order compelling the Manager of the National Bank of Commerce branch holding FAL accounts to pay the Chairman of the Labour Tribunal a sum equal to 18 months' salary which would be subsequently handed to me.

2 September 1986
There was a hearing in the High Court Chambers of Arusha, in which the General Manager of FAL sought and was granted leave to file an application for orders of certiorari (defined on page 93). His objective was to have the PLT Award quashed on grounds that the Labour Tribunal lacked jurisdiction. The General Manager of FAL relied on the provisions of Section 27(1) of the PLT Act which stipulates:

> Every award and decision of the Tribunal shall be final and shall not be liable to be challenged, reviewed, questioned or called into any court, *save on grounds of lack of jurisdiction.* (*my emphasis*)

As soon as leave was granted by the High Court, the General Manager, assisted by counsel from Tanzania Legal Corporation, filed another application, not for orders of certiorari, but for a stay of execution order under Miscellaneous Civil Application No. 119 of 1986. His intention was to secure an injunction that would not only prevent my reinstatement, but also stop payment of my salary arrears!

The chamber summons filed under Section 95 of the Civil Procedure Code was received by my solicitor and we were directed to appear before the Judge in the High Court for the following purpose:

> Execution of the Award by the Permanent Labour Tribunal at Arusha on 8 August 1986 in Trade Inquiry No. 3 of 1986 *be stayed* pending the determination of *appeal* by way of orders of certiorari *lodged and now pending in this court.* (*my emphasis*)

The application was supported by the affidavit sworn by the General Manager of FAL. Its contents were as follows:

AFFIDAVIT

I, —— Christian, take oath and state as follows:

1. I am the General Manager of Fibreboards (Africa) Limited, the applicant in this application.
2. I am conversant with the facts I am about to depose.
3. On or about 8 August 1986 the Permanent Labour Tribunal gave an award re-engaging L. T. K. Mukurasi whom the Company had declared redundant on account of abolition of her office.
4. Upon reading the award I have noted that there are good grounds *for challenging the award by way of order for certiorari* and I instructed the Company's lawyers so to act. (*my emphasis*)
5. I have been notified by the said lawyers that proceedings have been instituted in the High Court for application for

orders of certiorari in Miscellaneous Civil Cause No. 130 of 1986, which application is still pending.

6. I have drawn a cheque in favour of the District Registrar, Arusha High Court, for the amount equal to entitlements under the award, and the same to be deposited as security and *I am willing to furnish further sums as security* if required. (*my emphasis*)
7. The company has no work to offer to the employee in the capacity she has been re-engaged or in any other capacity.
8. I undertake to abide by the result of *the appeal* and any order the Court may issue if stay of execution is granted. (*my emphasis*)

The affidavit was signed by the General Manager of Fibreboards (Africa) Limited.

The words italicised in paragraphs 4 and 8 provided the technical grounds on which the General Manager's application was ultimately quashed. The PLT Award is not appealable. The words italicised in paragraph 6 are meant to show the degree of conscientiousness displayed by the General Manager as a guardian of the company's finances. It is doubtful that he would have appeared so magnanimous if the sums involved had been coming from his own resources. Also, though the General Manager of FAL claimed to be sure of his facts, I doubted whether he was sure he was not being misled. The Tribunal's Award stated that I was being reinstated, not re-engaged!

To return to orders of certiorari for which the General Manager filed an application. Orders of certiorari have their roots in English history and are a writ directed to an inferior court of record commanding it to certify to the King or Queen in the High Court of Justice some matter of judicial character. They are therefore used to remove civil causes or indictments from an inferior court of record to the High Court, so that they may be better tried, or if there has been abuse or error, retried. In this case the Permanent Labour Tribunal is an inferior court of record and the General Manager wished to move the High Court to retry the matter.

When my solicitors received the chamber summons and the General Manager's affidavit they prepared a counter-affidavit which they filed with the High Court. We were informed that hearing of the application for stay of execution of the Award would take place in the High Court Chambers on 8 September 1986 at 9 a.m.

4 September 1986

I began to have a glimmer of understanding as to the game that the General Manager of FAL and his collaborators were trying to play. They wanted to use the provisions of Section 27(1) of the PLT Act to delay or frustrate my being reinstated. In other words, they aimed to make my victory a hollow one. There was an unmistakable similarity between my case and that involving 116 workers illegally declared redundant by the Tanzania–Zambia Railway Authority (TAZARA). The General Manager of TAZARA had unlawfully refused to reinstate the workers after being ordered to do so by the Labour Tribunal. Couching his opposition in accordance with the provisions of Section 27(1) of the PLT Act, he had managed to frustrate their reinstatement. The case had dragged on for four years as it went through the High Court and finally the Court of Appeal. The workers had finally been reinstated by the Court of Appeal after facing considerable economic hardship. The General Manager of TAZARA had thereafter been given a three-year prison sentence for failing to obey a lawful order of the Permanent Labour Tribunal.

I had no intention of letting my case drag on for that long. As far as I was concerned, the Labour Tribunal had complete jurisdiction over my case and I was determined not to let the General Manager get away with his move to make a travesty of justice. I decided to put my last card on the table in the hope of salvation. I wrote a letter to the Principal Secretary to the President who is also the Chief of the Public Service. The Principal Secretary had been recently appointed to office, following the installation in office of the second President of Tanzania in October 1985. I felt I had nothing to lose by casting the dice in this way. In fact I would have something to gain if he decided to view my case sympathetically. There had been a spate of speeches made by the new President which as usual had struck a note that provided me with grounds for appealing to the President's Office.

The opening words of my letter quoted the very first speech the new President had made after being sworn in, and which had been very well received by many Tanzanians:

> You should not accept victimisation, because if you do so you encourage your oppressors to victimise you even more . . . Leaders should be accountable. To be accountable means performing one's duties with due regard to the laws, rules and regulations of the country . . . Look for justice through

the existing channels. However, if after that you still feel you are unjustly treated, write to me. I will do my best to assist.

I went on to detail the background to my case and the legal steps I had taken, emphasising the findings of the Tribunal and the ruling of the Minister of Labour. I attached a photocopy of the whole text of the Ruling. I requested the Principal Secretary to observe the time that had elapsed during the investigatory and adjudicatory stages. I asked him to take into consideration the specific finding of the Tribunal that my dismissal had been motivated by malice, conspiracy and victimisation and not cost-reduction considerations. In addition I pointed out that I saw the actions of the two General Managers (TWICO and FAL) to be a continuation of their personal vendetta, waged against me long before I was dismissed. I ended by imploring him to ensure not only that justice would be done, but also that it would be seen to be done.

This time I did not make a trip to Dar es Salaam. I sent my letter by registered post and hoped for the best. If I did not receive the appropriate response, then it would be the High Court and the Court of Appeal for me. I was determined to exhaust the judicial system in my quest for justice.

At the same time I wrote a letter to the Principal Secretary in the parent ministry, the Ministry of Natural Resources and Tourism, detailing all the facts relevant to my case, questioning the role of the General Manager of TWICO in my dispute, and requesting that his ministry intervene as a parent ministry. I sat back and waited.

8 September 1986

We assembled in the High Court Chambers for a hearing of the application for stay of execution of an award. By this time my solicitor had still not received the copy of the application for orders of certiorari. This was rather irregular, because the application for the orders of certiorari formed the basis for the application for stay of execution. This was clearly stated in their summons, but it was not available to us at that date.

The application for stay of execution was going to be heard, this irregularity notwithstanding. My solicitor had no alternative but to confine his arguments to the application for stay of execution. He moved the court to consider preliminary objections concerning procedure and jurisdiction before the hearing of the application. His arguments were centred around three paragraphs of the counter-affidavit:

(a) that the honourable court has no jurisdiction to entertain and adjudicate upon this application, IN THE ALTERNATIVE AND WITHOUT PREDUDICE, to the foregoing points of objection in law.

(b) that the invocation of the inherent powers of the Court enunciated under the provisions of Section 95 of the Civil Procedure Code, Act No. 49 of 1966 was not proper in Law.

(c) that the remedy of appeal being sought in the pending determination of a purported appeal by way of orders of certiorari is both unfounded and misconceived in law.

As a non-lawyer, I appreciated the services of a professional in a situation such as this. While I knew the substance of the law, the procedural aspect was another matter. I am not conversant with the Civil Procedure Code, but from what my solicitor said in legal jargon that was at times beyond me, the applicants had filed their case under the section of the law that sought to move the High Court as an appellate court to challenge the Award of the Permanent Labour Tribunal. This, he said, was not proper in law.

The applicant's solicitor was given room to reply. It appeared that my solicitor's line of argument had thrown him into total disarray. The learned counsel from Tanzania Legal Corporation had great difficulty in challenging the objections raised by my solicitors. The hearing was adjourned until 11 September 1986.

9 September 1986

Up to this day I had continued to report for work daily although I was not assigned any duties. As far as my salary was concerned, I had accepted by now that it was going to be a long time before I received it. At about midday I received a phone call from home that my daughter was running a temperature. I requested a company sick sheet and left to take my daughter to hospital. When I reached home my young daughter's condition was no better so I decided to phone the office to let them know that I might be back later than I had expected as I needed to make the child comfortable. It was very difficult for me to communicate with the telephone operator because there was a lot of noise in the background. She asked me to hold on so that she could see what was happening.

When she came back, it was still very difficult for us to communicate. In the end I decided to go back to the factory to see what was happening once my daughter had fallen asleep. When I arrived, however, I found that I could not get into my office. The noise I had heard had been made by the company carpenter who, I was informed, had been ordered by the General Manager to break my old lock and install a new one. In the presence of the JUWATA representative and the Party Chairman I tried the key to my office, demonstrating that it did not fit the new lock.

The General Manager's action was not only irregular but illegal as well. To my understanding he was committing a lock-out, which is an offence under Section 11 of the PLT Act. Moreover, his application for a stay of execution had not yet been heard by the High Court and he had no legal grounds for locking me out of my office. His action constituted not only contempt of the PLT Award but also disobedience of a lawful order.

10 September 1986

On this day the company vehicle did not come to my house as was the normal practice. I deduced quite correctly that the company driver had been ordered not to collect me. This was later confirmed by the driver himself. Accordingly, I did not report for work but visited the Regional JUWATA Secretary for advice and action. The Regional Secretary wrote to the Secretary General of JUWATA informing him of this new development, requiring him to take action at the highest level.

11 September 1986

We convened for the adjourned hearing of the application for orders for a stay of execution in the High Court Chambers. My solicitor had still not received a copy of the application for orders of certiorari. This time the applicant, FAL, couched its application in terms of Order 39, Rule 5 of the Civil Procedure Code and not Section 95 of the same code. FAL sought the High Court in its appellate jurisdiction to challenge the Award of the Permanent Labour Tribunal and also, pending its appeal, sought an order for a stay of execution.

My solicitor's argument was that by virtue of the finality clause under the Permanent Labour Tribunal Act the court was incompetent to entertain any appeal against the PLT. Correspondingly, he pointed out, there could be no question of entertaining an application for a stay of execution based on the purported appeal. Moreover, under the new amendment of the PLT Act the question of stay of execution did not arise. According to this amendment, Section 27(3),

> . . . every award shall be binding on the employers and employees to whom it relates, and may be enforced in any civil court of competent jurisdiction as if it were a decree of that court, notwithstanding that it has not yet been published in the Gazette, or that any of the parties has a right or is intending to file an action in any court on the grounds referred to in sub-section 1.

My solicitor's arguments took two and a half hours.

12 September 1986
I sought legal advice to establish the possibility of taking action against the General Manager for breaking into my office and locking me out. My solicitor agreed and drafted me a complaint which I took to the police station requesting the immediate arrest of the General Manager of FAL for disobeying a lawful order contrary to Section 124 of the Penal Code, Chapter 16 of the Laws. I duly took with me the certificate of the PLT Award and filed a criminal charge against the General Manager of FAL under file no. AR/RB/7449/86. I wrote a statement, signed it, and waited for some action to take place.

20 September 1986
No action had been taken by the police despite several attempts to get them to act. I decided to report back to my lawyer. My lawyer wrote to the Regional Police Commander, to enquire why the machinery for maintaining law and order was failing to take the necessary steps against the General Manager of FAL. The reply was that it was not a matter for the police to enforce the Awards of the Permanent Labour Tribunal. They asked us to approach the Resident Magistrate's Court to give them an order. By implication the order of the Permanent Labour Tribunal did not constitute a lawful order!

23 September 1986
The alternative was to file a complaint with the Resident Magistrate's Court according to Section 128 of the Criminal Procedure Code. I filed two complaints with the Resident Magistrate's Court against the General Manager of FAL. My aim was to carry out a private prosecution since the police would not act. The first complaint charged him with disobeying a lawful order, contrary to Section 124 of the Penal Code. The second charge against the General Manager of FAL charged him with participating in, and

inciting others to, a lock-out, contrary to Sections 11 and 12 of the PLT Act. I requested the Magistrate to issue an arrest warrant in the personal names of the General Manager of FAL who would subsequently be brought before the court to answer these criminal charges. It was imperative that the summons be issued in the General Manager's personal names, because a General Manager as such is an abstract entity. It was important to differentiate between the individual and his office. It was a person who was disobeying the order and not the abstract entity called 'the General Manager'.

24 September 1986
The order requiring the General Manager of FAL to report to the court was issued and served on him.

28 September 1986
It was gratifying to see the General Manager of FAL standing outside the Resident Magistrate's Court waiting to have a charge read to him. No longer the hunter but now one of the hunted, for once in the lifetime of this vendetta he was on the receiving end. He was not formally charged, however, because the Magistrate advised me to seek the consent of the Director of Public Prosecutions in order to carry out a private prosecution on behalf of the republic as is required under the law.

9 October 1986
The judgment for the orders of stay of execution of an award was read in the High Court Chambers. The Judge agreed with my solicitor that the High Court was not competent to entertain appeals to challenge decisions or awards of the Permanent Labour Tribunal. Accordingly, the General Manager's application for a stay of execution was struck out with costs awarded against FAL. Since it had lost its case on a technicality, FAL was given leave to file a fresh application, if it wished to do so. Its failures had simply begun.

17 October 1986
The Principal Secretary in the President's Office replied to my letter! In his letter which was addressed to the General Manager and copied to me, the Principal Secretary directed the General Manager of FAL to reinstate me immediately and to pay me all that I was entitled to. He also cautioned him to heed the country's laws and regulations and the decisions that are meant to enforce those laws and regulations.

There was no response from the Principal Secretary in the Ministry of Natural Resources and Tourism.

18 October 1986
The General Manager of FAL filed a fresh application, praying for a stay of execution of an award, with the High Court. We were summoned to appear at the High Court Chambers on 22 October 1986.

20 October 1986
I reported for duty with a copy of my letter from the Principal Secretary. The General Manager had left for Dar es Salaam. I suspected he had left to consult personally with his boss, the General Manager of TWICO.

26 October 1986
The General Manager, who had returned from Dar es Salaam, wrote me a letter in which he informed me that I was being re-engaged in accordance with the Principal Secretary's directive. He further informed me that the details and summary of my duties were being worked out. In the meantime the Finance and Administrative Manager was directed to pay me my salary arrears and to grant me 28 days' annual leave immediately. After my leave, I would have to report to the Finance and Administrative Manager who was to assign me duties. Finally, I was asked to take note that the application for orders of certiorari that was still filed with the High Court would be pursued until a decision was made.

What this letter seemed to imply was that I would not be reinstated in the position of Finance and Administrative Manager as the Tribunal had ordered. I was to report to the Finance and Administrative Manager who would assign me duties. This Finance and Administrative Manager of FAL had been recruited by TWICO and posted to FAL to replace the expatriate whose contract had expired earlier than envisaged. This was in clear contravention of the Tribunal's order. The recruitment of this man was precisely designed to frustrate my reinstatement in that position. During the PLT hearing there had not been any mention of a *new* Finance and Administrative Manager. Our arguments had been opposed to the earlier employment of an expatriate Finance and Administrative Manager. Secondly, it seemed my presence was an irritant to the General Manager, who virtually gave me compulsory leave. I did not need much shoving nor was I in a mood to argue. I needed time to recoup my strength after the hard struggle and also for the hard task which I felt was still ahead of me. I still had the inspiration, but the mission was not yet complete. The war was not yet won. My leave entitlement was for 56 days; I decided that I would take 40.

Finally, I had been warned that the application for orders of certiorari would remain pending until decided, the Principal Secretary's letter notwithstanding! I wondered whether the General Manager thought he was challenging my reinstatement or the Principal Secretary's directive, and how he would present the Principal Secretary's letter in court.

28 October 1986

Three events took place on this day. In the morning I was given an office, not in the Administrative office block, but in the unit that houses the door and clogs factory. This office was noisy and dusty and was normally used by the door factory foremen to store their tools and papers. I decided not to complain. On the same day I received a letter from the General Manager which said:

> *Re: Rumour-mongering and Loitering*
> I have to write to you to warn you against rumour-mongering and lack of discipline which has taken place since you were reinstated. You should not visit the office of the Party during office hours or I shall take disciplinary steps against you. You should also not loiter round during office hours.
>
> You are hereby being warned and I would like to emphasise that your being reinstated does not give you freedom to do anything you like.

In the afternoon the General Manager convened a meeting of the Management team, the Party and the Union. From the letter that was copied to me by the Chairman of the Party, the meeting was meant to deter all persons concerned from associating with me. The Chairman of the Party, who came from the same region as myself, claimed in his letter of complaint to the District Party Office that the General Manager had threatened to declare a tribal war against him.

30 October 1986

I wrote a letter to the General Manager, challenging him to substantiate the allegations made in his letter of 28 October 1986 by citing specific examples. I also requested him to put what had happened behind him so that we could get on with our work. He did not reply to my letter.

3 November 1986
I went on leave for 40 days. While on leave I learnt that the cheque which the Chairman of the Tribunal had demanded be endorsed to him had been sent not to the Tribunal, but to the Legal and Trustee Department of the National Bank of Commerce Headquarters in Dar es Salaam. So, if there had not been the timely intervention by the Principal Secretary, two cheques in my name would have been floating around: one with the High Court in Arusha and the other with the Legal and Trustee Bank of the National Bank of Commerce. It left me in no doubt as to how far the General Manager of FAL and his collaborators wanted to go to tighten the financial noose around my neck!

15 December 1986
I reported for duty. I went back to my noisy, dusty office in the door and clogs factory. I was not assigned any duties and I was determined not to make waves. I decided to change what would have been a totally frustrating experience into a useful pastime. I began to write the story of my struggle, the result of which is this book.

22 December 1986
I was given my old office in the administrative block. However, I was not assigned any duties. I continued to write.

29 December 1986
I received a letter from the Finance and Administrative Manager instructing me to register my movements in and out of the factory.

2 January 1987
I was given a job description by the Finance and Administrative Manager. According to this I had been designated Training Officer. This was the position I had held eight years ago, prior to my going to Manchester to obtain the postgraduate diploma in Personnel Management! My preliminary investigation revealed that there were 83 new employees since my dismissal under cost reduction.

8 January 1987
I wrote a letter to the Principal Secretary of the President's Office to seek clarification in view of the new duties to which I was being

assigned which, I felt, contravened the terms of the PLT Award. According to Section 27(3):

> No application to vary any Award shall except with the written permission of the Minister be made within twelve months of the date of the publication in the Gazette of such award . . .

The General Manager did not seek to vary the terms of the Award, which stated that I was to be reinstated as Personnel Officer until the position of Finance and Administrative Manager became vacant. In fact, he desired to have the whole Award quashed. It was clear that the General Managers of both TWICO and FAL had already ensured that the position would never be vacant since they had already installed someone in that position.

On the other hand, the position of Training Officer is junior to that of Finance and Administrative Officer, the position that is at the moment held by my former junior. So in effect he is now my senior. I am still awaiting clarification from the Principal Secretary.

The Struggle Continues!

PART FOUR

Lessons and conclusions

9

As I look back to the experience of my dismissal and reinstatement, the long period of struggle and moments of hopelessness by which it was marked, I am able to discover in it aspects which now form the basis for the conclusions and summing up of my case study. Not only were there lessons to be learnt by me but there are lessons relevant to the plight of women (and men) everywhere who may be caught up in a situation like mine. Though a nation's laws may be just, only with the greatest vigilance and the will to fight back against the injustices constantly inflicted on the powerless by the more powerful, on the weak by the strong, and by making these injustices public can any real changes be achieved. Although as a woman I felt that patriarchal values were working in conjunction with the austerity measures demanded by the economic crisis existing in Tanzania to ensure that it was I of all the managers who would be dismissed, other issues raised by my case have a more general relevance to all members of the labour force. Indeed, some of the issues raised encompass the way society operates as a whole. Although I write as a Tanzanian, members of other nations may find echoes of problems they too have experienced.

The issue of accountability has perplexed me. If accountability means being answerable to a superior or to a senior authority for commissions or omissions then my case raised serious questions. One month after my reinstatement by the Permanent Labour Tribunal I was locked out of my office and prevented from entering the company premises. These acts were illegal and in contempt of the order made by the Labour Tribunal. It puzzles me that, confronted with an order from the President's Office, an employee of a state-owned enterprise could act in contempt of that order and yet still keep his job. To whom was this employee accountable? What are the long-term consequences of such an action in terms of employee morale and motivation on the one hand and managerial responsibility and accountability on the other, virtues which the country's leadership has been exhorting us to adopt?

Another aspect of the issue of accountability related to the fact that the Tribunal found that my dismissal was due to victimisation. Why was no one held accountable for thus abusing his position? And who should be held accountable for the costs incurred in the conduct of the inquiry and payment of my salary arrears at a time of national economic stringency? Which instrument of government is responsible for holding certain persons accountable and why does it fail to act?

Whatever the answers to these questions, failure to take action will mean a continuation and indeed an escalation of such acts. If collusion lies behind acts of victimisation against the individual then I shudder to imagine the consequences of collusion involving, for instance, a plan to deprive the Government of millions of dollars through dubious transactions orchestrated at various levels of the bureaucracy.

In the course of my case I also observed failings in the Permanent Labour Tribunal Act, an extensive piece of legislation of which I would not pretend to make a critique. It has certain shortcomings, however, to which I should like to draw attention:

1. The time taken to process a dispute is so long that an aggrieved employee might well be deterred from seeking his or her rights.
2. The Act limits itself to a narrow area of employment and does not provide for all the other areas such as housing and other employee benefits. The issue of housing, for example, must be dealt with by another court.
3. The question of economic support during the period of a trade dispute is not addressed.
4. Managerial employees may find it difficult to get Union support, yet the definition of the case as a trade dispute is dependent on this.
5. The enforceability of the Tribunal Awards seems precarious.
6. Unscrupulous employers may find excuses for delaying or frustrating the implementation of justice due to uncertainty as to whether or not the Tribunal's Awards are final. Under some sections of the Act, the Minister of Labour's decisions with regard to labour disputes are said to be final. Under another section the disgruntled party in an Award may institute action in the High Court by merely claiming that the Minister lacked jurisdiction. It was this provision which made it almost possible for the same law to be used to prevent the implementation of the Minister's order

to reinstate me. The Minister of Labour is the President's representative on employment matters, yet at best he seems to have power without any teeth.

It would be erroneous to give the impression that I was the only personnel manager to lose her job during the cost-reduction exercise. Indeed, when I went for interview at Tanzania Textile Corporation and subsequently at Tanzania Audit Corporation (I was rejected for the post of Personnel and Training Officer), I met fellow personnel managers with whom I had struck up acquaintance during the annual Personnel Managers' Symposium who were also looking for jobs. Some of them had reached positions as directors, some like me were managers, others had officer rank. Most held at least one university degree.

These chance meetings set me wondering whether the personnel management function had a future in Tanzania. Was it pure accident that in the managerial ranks, personnel managers proved to have the greatest number of casualties arising from the cost-reduction exercise? Financial managers and chief accountants, for instance, did not appear to have met the same fate. In fact in a number of parastatal concerns there was a merger between the Finance and Administration Departments with the financial specialist emerging with the status of head of department and enjoying direct access to the top decision-maker. The personnel specialist, on the other hand, became a subordinate of the finance specialist and she or he was merely a head of section within the newly formed department, only communicating with the top decision-maker through a manager who had no experience or training in personnel matters.

It is a contradiction and unacceptable that this should happen in a socialist country where the political ideology espouses the supremacy of labour over all other factors of production. Indeed, the interests of the workers seem to have been placed below financial considerations.

This turn of events, of course, reflects in part the manner in which the personnel management function is viewed in Tanzania. There is a tendency in some circles to take the function for granted and to see it as something which can be done by almost any member of the organisation. It is not uncommon to find in the checkered composition of the group of current personnel directors, managers and officers, failures from other departments and institutions given a last chance by being transferred into the personnel office. Others have training as primary school teachers or only hold a certificate in book-keeping, word processing or some other subject unrelated to personnel management. There is no recognition of the fact that personnel management is a specialism in its own right, little appreciation of the need for personnel managers to be properly trained and experienced for a job that carries a responsibility for the welfare of the whole organisation. Appointment to the post of personnel manager should be strictly on merit. The personnel management function should be accorded the same status as financial and technical functions if political rhetoric is to be believed.

Bringing together, now, the various strands in my story I believe there are five important lessons from which much can be learnt by all those who fight victimisation:

Lesson number one

Women are victimised, not because of their womanness, but because of what men in their respective circumstances, whether in an office, family or cultural setting, think or regard womanness to represent. It should be clear by now that the reason I was dismissed was not necessarily because I am a woman. But, of course, neither did my being a woman confer on me any advantages or privileges. The main reason for my dismissal was that there were very basic and fundamental differences between myself and certain individuals who were in more powerful positions. It is possible that, even had I been a man, because of these differences I would have been dismissed under the cloak of the so-called 'national interest'.

What proved to be discriminatory against me as a woman was the particular set of circumstances surrounding my dismissal. The principle of First In, Last Out, for example, was completely disregarded and this made it possible for the company to retain a male employee who had served the company for fewer years. Secondly, the fact that the company's departments had been rationalised and merged to form four departments instead of seven meant that three heads of departments or managers should have been dismissed when their posts were abolished. However, I was the only woman manager at Fibreboards and the only manager to be dismissed, while the other heads of departments, who were men, were absorbed in other departments within Fibreboards. Finally, there was the lesser cause – the estrangement from my husband and the entanglement of my domestic life with my employment rights (or the use of informal factors to affect my formal rights). In my estimation this factor had a precipitating effect but was mainly incidental. I do not dismiss it completely but neither do I see it as the main cause. There is a proverb in my tribe which says: '*Nochuma atandamile*', literally meaning, 'You are pushing a squatting man.' He cannot do anything but fall. The person who ordered my dismissal did not need to be pushed. He had already propelled himself to jump.

In my view, my dismissal was seen as justified because, according to the powers that be, I did not behave as a woman should. I was no doubt seen as a troublemaker because I would not give the kind of advice that my superiors wanted to hear, and nor would I obey blindly the orders given by my superiors. My scrupulous observance of procedures did not necessarily endear me to my bosses or to my colleagues. I do not believe that there is a phenomenon called a female manager or male manager, and I felt I was entitled to take a certain stand on matters that I strongly believed in. I did not conform to the female stereotype which sees women as docile, passive and timid. Had I conformed this would have put me in the good books of my superiors. Firmness, decisiveness and truthfulness are undoubtedly not seen as desirable attributes in a female manager. I feel that the reason I was not dismissed for adopting a certain stand on things I believed in, until some people saw cost reduction as their excuse, was that the reasons I gave were normally legally sound. As such it would have proved highly embarrassing to dismiss me for insubordination lest I decided to challenge my dismissal.

That apart, there was a spurious moral justification for my dismissal. The fact that I was separated from my husband obviously put me in a certain category socially. The people intent on dismissing me did not want to know why this had happened, at least not from my side, and I was their employee. They were ready to listen and acknowledge and act on hearsay from the other side, but not to accord me a similar privilege. Thus the powers that be decided to be judge and jury and acted on the basis of what had been presented ex-parte. Being a member of the 'weaker' sex in the sexual hierarchy, without a husband, with every other employer implementing the same austerity measures, and now with my fall-back position swept from under my feet, it was clear to me what type of career I was being condemned to. I have no doubt no one expected me to challenge my dismissal, let alone to challenge it successfully. Womanness in this case was taken to mean weakness and helplessness but these were not, I believe, inherent attributes of my personality, make-up or circumstance. I do not subscribe to notions of females as weak. Women may be disabled by imposed socially constructed values but they are certainly not innately feeble.

Lesson number two

In most cases women who are victimised do not fight their way out because they think they cannot win. This has many causes. In the first instance, women (and men) are victims of patriarchal values, the values of the dominant group. The socialisation process instils notions of weakness, passivity and dependence in the female, and notions of courage, strength and self-reliance in the male. It inculcates and fosters an ideology based on the myth of male superiority and female inferiority. As is usual with all types of brainwashing, some women (and some men) come to believe what they are told without question. Myth comes to be regarded as reality. Thus it is said, 'A woman cannot win', and women come to believe that they cannot successfully challenge and confront men even on issues concerning their individual rights.

As many women who have had to struggle for their rights very well know, there is nothing inherently strong about men. What is seen as their strength, which in this case is synonymous with power, is not God-ordained but socially constructed and, like everything else that is socially given, capable of being subverted. Men, for example, are socialised and politicised into dealing in underhand ways, and are also versed in the art of political intrigue and manipulation. They have operated in the public sphere for longer and learnt the tools of the trade through the informal network long before women came into the picture. But this does not mean that men are inevitably a match for women who have studied and perfected their technique and also acquired some expertise in the male way of doing things. If such a man and woman were given an equal chance to fight for their rights, operating by the same rules, it is doubtful that a man would necessarily come out the winner. But what normally happens is that men do not play according to the rules. When a man is thus challenged, he resorts to tactics that look like hitting below the belt – calling upon a formal or informal male network of former schoolfriends and acquaintances and combining forces in order to get the upper hand. Having thus operated from a position of advantage he may turn around and glorify the myth of male supremacy and female inferiority.

When a woman decides to break the chains of her oppression, victimisation and degradation, on the other hand, she discovers that she is not fighting against the actions of the individual husband or employer. She discovers that she is fighting against a significant portion of the patriarchal superstructure in which men gang up together and use their positions against her as a single woman in order to destroy her. In other words it becomes a political struggle.

Unfortunately a woman does not possess the advantage of the informal network that is at men's disposal. Very few women are in positions of power and influence that a female militant can call upon, occupying as they do subordinate, marginalised or dependent positions in the patriarchal bureaucratic structures of the state. But even when women do possess power and influence, their assistance cannot be taken for granted. Being a woman does not imply the automatic possession of a feminist consciousness.

Another reason why women do not always fight is their lack of faith in a legal system that is predominantly composed of men. In my case, too, I found the prospect of struggling against so many men through a legal system controlled by men highly daunting. However, I also had a view and a faith that the men who have to dispense justice act as individuals and that some of them possess a strong commitment to the principles of fairness and justice. In my opinion, it would be grossly unfair and would prove disadvantageous for women to dismiss the judicial system as unjust simply on the grounds of its male-biased composition. In any case this composition is not likely to change in the near future.

The fact that I got reinstated through the male-dominated structures of JUWATA, the Permanent Labour Tribunal and the President's Office clearly negates this view. What I am saying, however, is not that favourable attitudes on the part of the people who have to dispense justice should be assumed or taken for granted, but that the judicial system should not be spurned without being tested. One should adopt an open mind on this issue.

A woman can win provided she has grounds and is willing and committed to the struggle. The decision to struggle for one's rights has to be an act of will.

Lesson number three

For a protracted struggle of this kind, the struggling individual woman (or man) should have material and moral support. It is of the utmost importance that she should be able to secure an income while the struggle continues. Without economic support, the individual may break down or end up as a beggar or a prostitute. In countries like Tanzania where there is no social security, there is a need to create some mechanisms for providing such support – through, for example, JUWATA or professional organisations. A fund should be created for this purpose. Once these organisations think that their member has a cause to complain they should offer financial and material support. This is a critical factor for every worker, man or woman. Moral support, which is the support of one's friends, colleagues, peers and family is also important. As far as I am concerned, my dismissal was enough to paralyse and incapacitate me. In fact, I don't doubt that it was calculated to destroy me totally. At the time of my dismissal I was separated from my marital home and was struggling to build my life afresh. My dismissal meant a double struggle – a struggle to survive and a struggle to get reinstated. I had no close relatives in Arusha since my parents are resident in a different part of the country. At the same time, in 1985, inflation was at its peak and I was being thrown out of the company house. I could easily have become destitute and a mental wreck.

What saved the day was that I was able to use what knowledge I had to my advantage and had established a considerable network of friends within and outside my country who gave me emotional and moral support. Because of my involvement with women's issues, I was invited to several meetings, conferences and workshops, locally and abroad, which mostly proved to be paid trips. These greatly enhanced my economic well-being. I was also able to take jobs of a temporary nature as a consultant or to present papers or give talks for a fee.

In terms of moral support the greatest and the most prized and touching contributions came from the workers at FAL and the Danish Volunteers who used to visit me occasionally and provide me with maize, rice and bananas or beans. They would drop by from time to time to check on me and enquire how my case was progressing. Their support was most encouraging. Friends, both near and far, used to telephone me or call on me to take me for a drink. My lawyer friends enlightened me on the procedural side of my case; other friends would volunteer financial support. The combination of all these kept me going.

Lesson number four

Ignorance of one's legal rights and a lopsided appreciation of the political system may hinder women (and men) from winning their cases or from even attempting to struggle. It is very sad that some people tend to place either too much or too little faith in the institution of justice and the political system. It was heartbreaking for me sometimes to hear people say in Kiswahili: '*hata ukilalamika, malalamiko yako yatafika wapi*?' which means, 'Even if you appeal against your dismissal, what kind of result can you hope to achieve?' These people evidently felt sure that I was going to lose the case. The instruments of justice were not perceived as an impartial arbiter between myself and my more powerful adversaries.

In a way, I could understand this perception but I was willing and ready to test my hypothesis that law can be impartially administered, provided that the individuals who have to deal with a particular case, and the system under which one petitions, are not inherently unjust. It is true, however, that I also knew what I wanted to achieve and to a certain extent how to go about it. When I was not sure of my ground, I simply groped in the dark. The Women's Organisation in Tanzania needs to work very hard in this area to provide and equip women with information and knowledge on their rights and increase their capability to handle struggles of this and other kinds.

Lesson number five

Struggles of this kind have to be publicised to enable other women to learn from them. It is said in the Bible that one's light should not be hidden under a bushel. Women have to make visible their struggles, their concerns, their fears and their hopes, since these contain the potential for transforming their lives. Struggles of this kind have long-term implications for the position of women in society. We should realise that silence does not enhance our liberation but has in fact kept us subjugated, oppressed, subordinated and divided. It is our isolation within ourselves, even when we are operating in the public sphere, that still fosters our humiliation and victimisation. It is our misguided fear of exposing what we consider to be 'private' that makes each woman feel a person apart. By publicising our problems, we may discover that we have more in common than we have differences. The experience bonds us together in the realisation of our common situation. We have another saying in Kiswahili: '*fimbo ya mnyonge ni kulalamika*', which means, 'Making matters public is the best weapon in the arsenal of the oppressed.' Women should realise that they have to bring what they see as their 'private' concerns into the public eye in order to demand change.

Publicising our struggles is a necessary condition for destroying the stereotype of women as weak and it may greatly assist in bringing the social ideology which sees females as inferior more into line with the political ideology which promotes ideals of equality. The lessons to be learnt from making public our struggles may not only help policy formulators and implementors to reassess existing policies but also assist in putting into practice what is already written on the equality agenda, which was meant to enhance the position of women. Women have to assist in furthering the good intentions of the benevolent patriarchy, limited in content and scope as the existing policies and laws are, by meeting these efforts halfway. It is my hope that this case study will stimulate more struggles, successes and publications of this kind.

10

It is August 1987 and I have written the final part of my story in Brighton, at the University of Sussex. I came here as a tutor on the course entitled 'Women, Men and Development' at the Institute of Development Studies. My recruitment came about as the result of a chance suggestion by a friend in Tanzania who had attended the course the year before. Not imagining that anything would come of it, but realising that I had nothing to lose, I sent in my application and was delighted to find that it was successful.

The course on Women, Men and Development is held every 15 months to two years and lasts for three months. In 1987 participants came from 17 Third World countries: eleven from Asia, five from Latin America and eight from Africa. The aim of the course is to broaden understanding of the role gender plays in determining participation in economic, social and political activities. The sessions on structural adjustment policies and their implications for women struck home forcibly. So nearly had I become a casualty of the austerity measures imposed under these policies!

Such an opportunity could not have come at a better time. The course enabled me to get a clearer perspective on my case by talking about it with course participants and colleagues on the team. Some aspects of my case that I had not thought out properly before were brought into sharper focus and I was helped to refine my thinking and writing.

At the Institute for Development Studies I met some of the most outstanding people working in the field of gender and development, in particular Kate Young, the Course Director, and the Co-Directors, Naila Kabeer and Faustina Ward-Osborne. I attended many lectures and met individuals with considerable experience in the areas of concern raised by my case and who have thought deeply and written much on the woman question. Without a doubt this whole experience has broadened my outlook and taught me much.

When it came to my asking my employers for seven months' unpaid leave of absence from the firm to act as tutor on the course,

I was astounded by the response. Not only was my release granted but simultaneously another letter was sent to SCOPO confirming that Management blessed my release and that they hoped that SCOPO would render me the necessary help to allow me to proceed to the Institute. With this acceptance in principle the rest was easy. My recruitment was sponsored by the Commonwealth Secretariat. The General Manager of TWICO, whose signature was required to secure the travelling clearance from the State House, treated me with the utmost courtesy when I went to visit him. In general there seemed to be tremendous goodwill surrounding my trip to Britain.

Before I left Tanzania many wellwishers came to see me. What the men said was interesting and encouraging:

> What you went through is enough to discourage any valiant heart even if it was possessed by a man. Very few men will persist and endure in the same way that you did. As you notice, there are very few individuals who have decided to take their cases before the Tribunal, even if they knew they were being victimised. You are not a woman. You are a man in a woman's form!

What the women said inspired me to believe that it had all been worthwhile:

> Laeticia, you have showed us the way. You have showed us that even a woman, when she is determined, can win and force people to act. From now onwards we intend to follow your example.

POSTSCRIPT

JANUARY 1990

I am now the Manpower Development and Administrative Manager at Fibreboards (Africa) Limited. The company has reverted to its old structure at the request of Management on the grounds that the structure adopted during the cost-reduction measures proved unworkable. We now have six departments instead of four and the Administration Department has been separated from the Finance Department.

Winning the acceptance of my superiors after my return from Sussex was not an easy matter, and as such I shall summarise the main occurrences. Serious attempts to frustrate and oust me were made. For a long time I remained in the position of Training Officer but no assignments were given to me and my attempts to get anything done were rebuffed. Forces within and outside the company nearly succeeded in isolating me from the JUWATA branch leadership and some members of the work force. On one occasion a request was made to the Board of Directors of TWICO and the State House that I be removed from the TWICO Group and transferred to the Ministry of Manpower Development and Labour for re-assignment, in order to defuse the situation at FAL and bring it back to normal management. Once, in June 1988, I was suspended on half pay and threatened with dismissal yet again, for 'failing to report for duty for a fortnight' at the time when I had the express permission of the General Manager to attend a Women Leaders' Workshop. I endured it all, made complaints to the relevant authorities when the pressure became unbearable, but mostly acted as if nothing was happening. I aimed at staying at FAL. This was one of the unhappiest periods of my struggle.

The resolution of our conflicts came finally from the concerted efforts of certain public offices and a change of attitude on the part of the individuals concerned. First was the Probe Team, led by the Chairman of the Board of TWICO, which visited FAL in April 1988. It did a commendable job and came out with many recommendations. Noteworthy was its recommendation that we all open a new page and start afresh. Then there was positive intervention by the Ministry of Land, Natural Resources and Tourism which took timely action to reinstate me after my suspension and urged my superiors to create an enviroment of understanding so as to avoid further conflict.

I was surprised when, late in June 1988, the General Manager of FAL called me into his office and told me that the conflict between us was over, and that, as we had been recommended to do, we should forget the past and start afresh. To confirm his good intentions, he convened a meeting comprising senior officials from the company, CCM and JUWATA to inform them of this decision. Most of those present had witnessed my struggle and were so astonished that they could only shake our hands and congratulate us. Finally, the General Manager met with members of my family and we shared food and drink in the true African tradition. My mother, who was the oldest person present, asked us to live like '*ndugu*' (Swahili for brothers) and this is exactly how we have lived ever since.

At the end of 1989 I had a private discussion with the General Manager and asked him why it had taken him so long to accept me after my reinstatement. His reply went back to the period prior to my dismissal. It seemed to indicate that his actions were the result of pressure exerted by his male colleagues and superiors who castigated him for 'harbouring a husband-deserter' after I separated from my husband. Then, when the award of the Permanent Labour Tribunal was announced, the same group had jeered at him for 'letting a woman win'. They told him that he must not let a woman get the better of him. Amidst all this confusion, he had sought the help and guidance of his superior, the General Manager of TWICO, without success. Then, as time went on, he had not found reasonable grounds for continuing the conflict and had decided to end it.

We now have a new Board of Directors whose Chairman is a university professor of economics. My old colleagues are still there but we have two new heads of department. The General Manager of TWICO has been relieved of his position and transferred to the Ministry of Land, Natural Resources and Tourism. The EKONO Project Manager has since completed his contract and left for Finland.

The atmosphere is much more agreeable now, and I work with renewed confidence. To begin with, my position was a given one; now I have a new, positive perspective of a position fought for and won.

In addition to these positive developments at the workplace, in January 1989 I was nominated by the Central Committee of the Party on to the Advisory Board of the Development of Administration of the National Executive Committee Secretariat. In June 1989, I was elected a member of the General Council of JUWATA.

Appendix

Legislation, policies and constitutional provisions affecting women's rights in formal employment in Tanzania

1. Employment Ordinance Cap 336

(a) This ordinance, in existence since colonial times, gives equal employment opportunity to both women and men in terms of wages, leave, holidays and termination of employment contracts. It also contains special provisions relating to women in employment such as:

- prohibition of women taking certain types of employment, for example in mines (section 86);
- prohibition of women working certain hours, that is, from 10 p.m. to 6 a.m. in any industrial undertaking (Section 83–(1)).

(b) Maternity Benefits under the law give the right to maternity leave of 56 days to all women employees, married or unmarried, once every three years (Section 25A as amended by Act No. 20 of 1975). In addition nursing mothers are entitled to half an hour twice a day during their working hours for the purpose of attending the baby (Section 25B of Act No. 20 of 1975).

2. Security of Employment Act Cap 574 (1964)

This is the law governing dismissals, terminations or redundancy, and applies equally to male and female employees. For details of the relevant section (6(1)g), see p. 45.

3. Government Standing Orders Section D 20 (1971)

According to this order, all employment is open to women who are suitably qualified. It prohibits differences between salaries or other terms of service of men and women employees of equivalent qualification and experience.

4. SCOPO Directive No. 44 of June 1981
This clarifies the State's position on fringe benefits for women workers in parastatal organisations. This directive instructs all employers in the state-owned enterprises to give travel allowance, housing facilities and medical services to all employees, male or female, without reference to their marital status.

5. The Party (CCM) Constitution (1987)
The Party creed Article 1, Section 4, states *inter alia* that:
(a) all human beings are equal;
(b) every individual has a right to dignity and respect;
(c) socialism and self-reliance is the only way of building a society of free and equal citizens.

Among the Party objectives are the following:
- to ensure that the Government and all public institutions give equal opportunity to all citizens, women and men alike, irrespective of race, tribe, religion or status;
- to ensure that there is no injustice, intimidation, racial discrimination, oppression or favouritism.

6. The Government Constitution (1988)
The main objectives as identified in Section 2.9(1) include provisions designed:
- to ensure that human rights are respected in accordance with the World Declaration of Human Rights;
- to ensure that the Government and its instruments give equal opportunity to all its citizens, men and women, regardless of race, tribe, religion or personal status.

Section 3, which addresses itself to the Government's main duties and obligations, states *inter alia* that:
- all human beings are born free and all are equal;
- no person may be discriminated against by another person or any other authority that is entrusted with the responsibility of implementing the law as an instrument of the State and of the Party.

7. The Permanent Labour Tribunal Act (1971)
This law empowers the PLT to carry out, among other functions, investigations and settlement of industrial disputes between employers and registered trade unions.

Bibliography

Blau, P., *Bureaucracy in Modern Society*, Random House, New York, 1965.

Charles, N., 'Women and Trade Unions', *Feminist Review*, 1986.

Chattopadhyay, G. P., 'The Identity of the Eastern African Manager: Some Implications for Management Education', in *Managerial Psychology* Vol. I, No. 1 (1980).

Croll, E., 'Rural Development in Transition to Socialism: practices and problems in the Soviet Union and China', Mimeo. Institute of Development Studies, University of Sussex.

Grindle, M. S., *Politics and Policy Implementation in the Third World*, Princeton University Press, 1980.

Guy Peters, B., *The Politics of Bureaucracy: A Comparative Perspective*, Longman, New York, 1978.

Lipumba, N. H. I., 'The Economic Crisis in Tanzania', in *Economic Stabilisation Policies in Tanzania*, National Workshop on Economic Stabilisation Policies in Tanzania, Dar es Salaam, January 1984.

Mapolu, H., 'The Organization and Participation of Workers in Tanzania, by H. Mapolu (ed.), *Workers and Management*, Tanzania Publishing House, Dar es Salaam, 1976.

Mascarenhas, O., and Mbilinyi, M., *Women in Tanzania: An Analytical Bibliography*, Scandinavian Institute of African Studies, Uppsala, Stockholm, 1983.

Ministry of Labour and Manpower Development, 'Annual Manpower Report to the President', 1981.

'Annual Manpower Report to the President', 1982.

Mihyo, P. B., *Industrial Conflict and Change in Tanzania*, Tanzania Publishing House, Dar es Salaam, 1983.

Molyneux, M., 'Mobilisation without Emancipation: Women's Interests, State and Revolution in Nicaragua', *Feminist Studies*, Summer 1985.

'Women's Emancipation under Socialism: A Model for the Third

World', Discussion Paper 151, Institute of Development Studies, University of Sussex, 1981.

Mtengeti, A. R., 'Women, Employment and the Law', paper written in preparation for the UN Women's Decade Conference, 1985.

Mukandalla, R. S., 'Bureaucracy and Socialism in Tanzania', in *The African Review: A Journal of African Politics, Development and International Affairs*, Vol. 10, No. 2 (1983), University of Dar es Salaam.

Mukurasi, L. T. K., 'Factors Inhibiting the Participation of Women at Senior Level in the Government and Parastatal Organisations', *Tanzania Business Review*, April 1984; *New Outlook*, No. 34, August/September 1984.

'Tanzania: Women, Socialism and Government's Basic Industrialisation Strategy', in *Women and the Industrial Development Decade for Africa*, Economic Commission of Africa, 1986.

Ndulu, B. J., 'The Structural Adjustment Programme in Perspective and Preliminary Implementation Evaluation', paper prepared for the seminar on Planning organised by DEVPLAN, Arusha, January 1984.

Ngomballe Mwiru, K., Keynote Address to the International Conference on the Arusha Declaration, Arusha, 1986.

Ngumbullu, P. J., 'The Structural Adjustment Programme Perspective', paper prepared for the seminar on Planning organised by DEVPLAN, Arusha, January 1984.

Nyalali, F. L., *Aspects of Industrial Conflict: A Case Study of Trade Disputes in Tanzania 1967–1973*, East Africa Literature Bureau, Nairobi, 1975.

Nyerere, J. K., *Freedom and Development*, Oxford University Press, London, 1973.

'The Arusha Declaration: Ten Years After', in *The African Review*, Vol. 7 No. 2, 1977, University of Dar es Salaam.

Pratt, C., 'Nyerere on the Transition to Socialism in Tanzania', *The African Review*, University of Dar es Salaam. Vol. 5, No. 1, 1975.

Rodney, W., 'Class Contradiction in Tanzania', in *The State in Tanzania*, by Haroub Othman (ed.), Dar es Salaam University Press, 1980.

Safilios-Rothschild, C., 'Women as Change Agents', in *Sex Roles and Social Policy*, by J. Lipman-Blumen et al. (eds.), Sage Publications, for the International Sociological Association (ISA), 1979.

Shimwela, N. N. P., 'Tanzania: Some Reflections on the Deepening Economic Crisis', in *Economic Stabilisation Policies in Tanzania*, National Workshop on Economic Stabilisation Policies in Tanzania, Dar es Salaam, January 1984.

Shivji, I. G., *Class Struggles in Tanzania*, Monthly Review Press, London, 1976.

Swantz, M. L., *Women in Development, a Creative Role Denied*, C. Hurst & Co., London, 1985.

Young, K., 'How to Integrate Women's Needs into Local, Regional and National Planning', Mimeo. Institute of Development Studies, University of Sussex.